# HE FILLS MY CUP

A 90-day devotional to refresh and restore your soul; drink from the fountain

Dennis L Taylor

RSI
PUBLISHING

Scriptures are taken from the English Standard Version of the Bible
Books may be ordered through booksellers or by contacting:
Dennis L Taylor
Taylord@parkavenue.org

RSIP-Charles Morris
https://www.rsiministry.com
Navarre, Florida

ISBN: 9798986448688
Printed in the United States of America
Edition Date: February 2023

# Contents

# Foreword

The world is full of junk food theology consumed in bits and pieces like a smorgasbord. Many students of God's word are surfers, riding the surface of living water seeking entertainment, self-help, or somewhere to excuse God's love and God's justice.

This book by Dennis Taylor is a rare opportunity to experience devotionals dealing with the pains and joys of daily personal experiences.

As you read *"HE FILLS MY CUP,"* one can tell this author has explored and charted the spiritual and emotional depths himself. You can almost hear King David crying out to the Lord in Psalms 139:23.

**Search me, O God, and know my heart! Try me and know my thoughts!**

In this book, Dennis is not sharing shallow teachings for those who suffer from short attention spans, or those who refuse to be provoked to spiritual transformation. *"HE FILLS MY CUP"* guides the reader through the Bible, painting beautiful word pictures that challenge us to face God's truth over worldly opinions. He addresses issues such as faith versus fear, and is the church "a culture" with moral influence, or has it become a powerless sub-culture that is out of sight and out of mind?

Taylor connects God's words, heart, and promises with His expectations and judgments. This book elevates the reader's understanding of our daily decisions to be either a victim to our circumstances or a servant to our Lord.

In reading this book, one can see that Dennis Taylor is passionate about the redeemed in Christ and the finished work of our Lord Jesus Christ in each of us. His heart cries to see the body of Christ purified on the inside while manifesting a visible testimony on the outside for the world to behold.

Every man and woman born again is unique, and God's Spirit and God's Word is transforming them into a New Creation in Christ. God's gift of grace in giving up His Son to die for humanity offers us the fantastic opportunity to explore the depths of God's Word and God's love. See the author's vision of what believers can expect in the days to come as *"HE FILLS MY CUP."* Who is this man? Take a deep breath, immerse yourself in the Lord Jesus and His promise of living water, and go deeper.

Charles Morris
Pastor, Author, and Publisher
Founder and CEO of RSIM and RSIP

# -1-
# A Thankful Heart

Thanksgiving is one of my favorite times of the year. It's exciting to have some time off, eat great food and hang out with family and friends. It is also a time to remind us to be thankful. It would do us so much good to hear this message more than once a year. Lord, give us a grateful heart. The quality of our lives, whether we love or hate it, is based on how thankful we are for God. Our attitude determines whether life is a place of blessing or misery. It all depends on our perspective and how we see things. If we want to find joy, we must first learn how to be thankful. Every time we grumble and complain, the quality of our lives is significantly reduced. When unthankful, we open the door for Satan to do his work.

How many of us need to repent from ingratitude? How many of us must tell someone, "I am sorry." Is there someone you need to forgive today?

*Psalm 100:4-5: "Serve the Lord with gladness; come before Him with joyful singing...Enter His courts with thanksgiving and enter His courts with praise. Give thanks to Him; bless His name. For the Lord is good and his love endures forever; and His faithfulness to all generations."*

The key that unlocks the gates of heaven is a thankful heart. Don't take life's blessings for granted.

*Challenge for today:* Break out the index cards and write down Psalm 100:4-5. Commit these verses to memory.

When negativity hits, say these verses repeatedly out loud. I also want to challenge you to list things you are thankful for and take the time to thank Him personally.

# -2-
# The God of the Valley

No matter what the enemy tells you today, Jesus Christ is the God of the mountains and the valley. Lock that into your memory bank, and never forget it. Nobody likes the valleys of life, but I am finding out that is where the fruit is produced. How did Jesus prepare to do His unbelievable works? Part of His training involved suffering. Think about it: He can serve as a faithful high priest because He suffered what we suffer. He understands what we go through. God wants to take our sorrows to enlarge our hearts. I love the story of Joseph. I want to encourage you to take the time and read Genesis 37-45. Joseph was betrayed by his brothers and sold into slavery. Potiphar's wife unjustly accused him. He was thrown in jail and forgotten by all except God. He faced some tough times. No matter what came Joseph's way, good or bad, he faithfully served God. He was continually tested, but he kept passing the test. Finally, God brought His plan together for Joseph's life at the right time.

God uses everything we go through for His glory and to fulfill His purpose. I will not pretend to understand why we must go through the valleys entirely, but we must remain faithful and keep His promises. The Lord used Joseph to touch the lives of thousands and thousands of people. As we stay loyal to Him during our trials, the character of Jesus Christ will emerge in our spirit, and He will be revealed to those around us. Stay faithful, my friend.

**Proverbs 18:10: "The name of the Lord is a strong tower; the righteousness runs into it and is safe."**

*Challenge for today:* Ask yourself these questions. Would your friends describe you as faithful? Why or why not? Would you describe yourself as a faithful servant of God? I want to challenge you today, whether you are going through good times or bad times, to stay loyal to the God of both situations. Know that He is there, and He will see you through.

# -3-
# What is Prayer?

What is prayer?

**1. Prayer is an act of dedication.**

*Luke 15:7: "If you remain in me and my words remain in you, ask whatever you wish, and it will be done."*

The less we talk with the Lord, the more dependent we become on ourselves. The more we pray, the less we depend on ourselves. Prayer is an act of communication. Poor communication causes enormous problems. Try not to talk with your spouse for a week. See how that works for you.

**John 15:15-16: "I no longer call you servants, because a servant does not know His master's business. Instead, I have called you friends, for everything that I learned from my Father I have made known to you. You did not choose me, but I chose you and appointed you so that you might go and bear fruit-fruit that will last. Then the Father will give you whatever you ask in my name."**

**2. Prayer is an act of supplication.**

*Philippians 4:6-7: "Do not be anxious about anything, but in everything, by prayer and petition, with thanksgiving, present your request to the Lord. And the peace of God, which transcends all understanding, will guard your heart and your minds in Jesus Christ." God never shuts the storehouse doors until we close our mouths. Go to your Father; He wants to hear from you.*

**3. Prayer is also an act of cooperation.**

*John 14:12-14: "I tell you the truth, anyone who has faith in me will do what I have been doing. He will do even greater things than these, because I am going to the Father. And I will do whatever you ask in my name, so that the Son may bring glory to the Father. You may ask me anything in my name, and I will do it."*

Wow, what a powerful verse. There are no limits when it comes to prayer. The Lord is pushing us to kick up our prayer lives. We can watch worry and stress disappear when we learn to trust Him. Let's grow in our prayer lives and watch how God will change our hearts and the lives of people around us. The God of miracles in the Bible is still the same God that lives in my heart today through the power of the Holy Spirit.

*Challenge for today:* Fall on your knees and get your hearts right with Him. Let us pray Heaven down and watch Satan shake. Believe in God's Word today. You can trust it.

# -4-
# First John 1:7

Have you ever had one of those mornings when you just wanted to go back to bed? I hate to say it, but that is what I feel this morning. It has been one of those weeks, but I look forward to partnering with God today. I am going ahead and keeping my eyes on Christ. Grab that cup of java, and jump into God's Word.

First, John 1:7 has jumped in my lap today like a hot cup of coffee. It has grabbed my attention, and it has me moving.

> *1 John 1:7: "But if we walk in the light, as he is in the light, we have fellowship with one another, and the blood of Jesus, His Son, purifies us from all sin."*

Christ indwells you. The blood of Jesus Christ purifies us from all sin. That is excellent news, but why all the guilt? Why all the regrets? Shouldn't we live with a smile and a sparkle in our eyes? The devil is the great accuser and is very good at it. He wants to distract us from our gaze on Christ and turn our attention to all the negativity around us.

We all occasionally fall to sin, but always remember that sin may touch you but cannot claim you if you are in Christ. Christ in you, the hope of all glory. Trust His work in you through the blood of Jesus. You may be walking through a rough time when everything isn't firing on all cylinders. It's like walking in the dark and hoping to see the light at the end of the tunnel. Will it ever come? I encourage you to remember that the King of kings loves you. He gave His only Son to die on a rugged cross. Jesus overcame sin and death and is seated at the right hand of God. If you are in Christ, you are on the winning team, and the hope of all glory lives in you.

*Challenge for today:* Walk in victory and not defeat. When all seems bleak, think about how blessed you are to have a Heavenly Father that has forgiven your sins. Hold first John 1:7 close to your heart, and don't let it go. "Thank the Lord for the Word of encouragement."

# -5-
# Drink

Growing up in Southwest Georgia, the summers were scorching. We always seem to gather at the community pool or make our homemade slip-and-slide. I was invited to the varsity football camp in the summer of my tenth-grade year. We had three practices a day and a weight workout because Coach Welsh was from the old school and did things his way. After lunch, training in full pads was the worst. It was closing in on 100 degrees every day, and there was no breeze. By the way, our practice uniform was not washed except once a week; imagine that smell. During that midday practice, we could only get water one time. Still, to this day, water never tasted so good, and they had to pull us away. We all need water to live; it is necessary, especially on days like this. I mentioned this memory to say this.

It's incredible how our body comprises about 80% fluids. We are a walking water balloon apart from the brain, bones, and a few organs. Stop drinking water and see what happens. It will affect your whole body. Our body needs water the same way a tire needs air. Deprive your soul of spiritual water, and your soul will scream out.

*John 7:37-38: "If anyone thirst, let him come to Me and drink. He who believes in Me, as the Scriptures has said, out of his heart will flow rivers of living water."*

What water can do for your body, Jesus can do for your heart. No directions are needed, but permission is required. Jesus won't come in unless you swallow. You can stand chest-deep in a pool and still die of thirst. Until you swallow, the water does you no good. Until we drink Christ, the same is true. Do you need a drink of Christ? Verse 37 is an invitation, and that invitation is to anyone. Religion pacifies but never satisfies. While church activities might hide the thirst, only Jesus can quench it. Drink of Him today.

**Revelation 22:17: "The Spirit and the bride say, 'Come.' And let him who hears say, 'Come.' Whoever is thirsty, let him come; and whoever wishes, let him take the gift of the water of life."**

Ceaseless fellowship with Christ satisfies a thirsty soul. Drink deeply and drink often.

*Challenge for today:* Stay hydrated spiritually. Come to Jesus daily and drink of Him. Open God's Word and dine on His written Word. Wash it down with close fellowship, and don't forget to swallow.

# -6-
# A Prayer for Protection, Guidance, and Forgiveness

David was a man after God's own heart. He was known for being a warrior and a king. However, David also had plenty of enemies and struggled with several temptations. David was smart enough to realize he needed help and couldn't do it alone. David wasn't afraid to pour out his heart to God. Some of the most powerful prayers ever recorded came from the lips of David. David prayed for three things in Psalms 25:1-7. The first thing David prayed for was protection from his enemies.

*Psalms 25:1-3: "To you, O Lord, I lift up my soul; in you Lord I Trust, O God. Do not let my enemies triumph over me. No one whose hope is in you will ever be put to shame."*

The second thing David prayed for was guidance.

*Psalms 25:4-5 David prays, "Show me your ways, O Lord, teach me your paths: guide me in your truth and teach me, for you are God my Savior, and my hope is in you all day long."*

David knew who was in control, and he knew the wisdom of the Lord. The third thing David prayed for was forgiveness.

***Psalms 25:7, "Remember not the sins of my youth and my rebellious ways; according to your love, remember me, for you are good, O Lord."***

Take time to read Psalms 51, where David pleaded with God to wash him clean and forgive him for his sin with Bathsheba. I don't know about you, but I need all the help I can get. David gives us a great example of a prayer we need to pray. Satan has kicked it up a notch because he knows his time is short, and he will do anything to destroy you. More than ever before, we need to turn to God in prayer and ask for protection, guidance, and forgiveness. Be authentic and upfront with the Lord and drop all pretense. "Lord, guard my family and me against the enemy. I pray for a hedge of protection as we stand for you. Father, I also pray for your wisdom. Lead, guide, and direct me in all my ways. Please help me to live a life that makes you smile. Cleanse me, O God, from all wrong. Forgive me when I failed you. Renew a steadfast spirit in me."

*Challenge for today:* Pray for protection, guidance, and forgiveness. Open your day with prayer, and never say amen till you lay your head on your pillow. Your day should be covered with constant prayer. Be in continuous communication with your Heavenly Father.

# -7-
# The Rescue and The Race

If you are in Christ, you have been rescued. You have been set free, forgiven, and placed in the family of God. But being a Christian involves more than a "rescue operation." There is a race to run and a purpose to fulfill. Take time to read 2 Timothy 1:8-9. Paul was writing to Timothy and telling him that you are rescued because of His grace and so that you might fulfill His purpose. The glory of our salvation experience seems to outshine the glory of God's original purpose in creating man. The rescue is the starting point of the race, not the finish line.

> **Hebrews 12:1: "Let us throw off everything that hinders and the sin that so easily entangles and let us run with perseverance the race marked for us."**

I encourage you to carry this verse in your heart all day. In other words, write it on paper, and stick it in your pocket or your purse. Read it repeatedly. Ask God throughout the day, "What does this mean to me, Lord?"

What is the race that God has marked for you? What is your calling and purpose in life? "Lord, awaken our hearts. Forgive us when we are consumed with our needs, problems, and projects. Wake up the souls of your church. Help us to run the race that You have marked for us. Please give us the endurance and discipline to finish the race well."

*Philippians 3:13-14: "Forgetting what is behind and straining towards what is ahead. I press on toward the goal to win the prize for which God has called me heavenward in Christ Jesus."*

Run through the tape. Finish strong.

*Challenge for today:* What is your strategy for running your best race? It would be best if you had a plan for how you will run this race called life. I encourage you to find a life coach who will work with you, pray, and push you to be more like Christ. Get together, see what God lays out, and then get it done. Give it your best effort and cross that line for His glory.

# -8-
# Fellowship Is a Privilege

I have always had massive respect for Billy Graham. Growing up, we only had three channels, but I remember Billy Graham coming on TV and preaching to a football stadium of people. He didn't mix words or try to sugarcoat things, but he presented the Gospel of Jesus Christ with power. I know I missed my chance to meet him, but I could imagine the excitement I would've had if I could have had a private appointment with him. Yet the God of the universe invites all His children for a private meeting and allows them to enter His presence for unrestricted fellowship. What a privilege.

Think about it; our God encourages us to spend time with Him, allowing us to know Him intimately and enjoy His presence. What a privilege. But that is not all. Our God has invited us to participate in accomplishing His eternal purpose. What a privilege. Life's ultimate freedom is wrapped up in one word: Fellowship.

> **Philippians 3:10: "I want to know Christ and the power of his resurrection and the FELLOWSHIP of sharing in his suffering, becoming like him in his death."**

Take advantage and enjoy the most incredible privilege you have on this earth. I know today is full of activities but take time to meet with the God of this universe. Let Him love on you. It's a privilege.

*Challenge for today:* Don't miss out on the privilege of a lifetime by skipping your daily time with the Father. Starting today, make your time alone with God your highest priority, and treasure this opportunity to dine and fellowship with royalty. Make sure today you have at least one person to hold you accountable for following through with this commitment.

# -9-
# Psalm 119:9-12

We live in a day when many Christians are being pulled away from their faith. In many cases, it's hard to tell believers from unbelievers.

**Deuteronomy 6:12 warns us, "Be careful that you do not forget the Lord."**

When we committed to following Christ, we decided to turn away from our old way of life. The decision was to do a complete 180-degree turn and follow hard after Christ. God has called us to a life of holiness and righteousness, not a life of being lukewarm where you are caught sitting on the fence.

**Proverbs 26:11: "As a dog returns to its vomit, so a fool repeats his folly."**

That is a gross verse, but it is full of truth. Imagine what the heart of God feels when His children return to their old life of sin. It must break God's heart when we push Him to the side and live a life that is all about us. Sometimes we even wonder, how did we get here? How did I fall so far from the Lord?

**Psalm 119:9-12 says, "How can a young man keep his way pure? By living according to your word. I seek you with all my heart; do not let me stray**

*from your commands. I have hidden your word in
my heart that I might not sin against you. Praise
be to you, O Lord; teach me your decrees."*

I will be the first to say it is not easy living the Christian life. It is a war, and Satan will do everything he can to discourage you and pull you away from that loving relationship with Christ. Please do three things this morning. First, identify Satan's tactics to distract your relationship with Christ. He uses tactics that he has used on you in the past. Be aware. Second, ask God to forgive you for straying away and ask Him for strength and wisdom. Third, get back to God's Word. Hide God's Word in your heart. Make it a top priority in your life. The Word of God is alive and active and will change your life.

*Challenge for today:* Let's get back on track. Recharge by amping up your time alone with God, and make sure your input is more significant than your output. Ask God for wisdom and discernment. We have a lot to do and many people to reach. Open your eyes to what He wants to show you.

# -10-
# Submit To the Will of God

God is good. All the time. I encourage you to read John 13:1-11. Jesus, the very Son of God, changed leadership forever. He willingly humbled Himself and bathed His disciple's feet. He took on the role of a servant. This act of humility had to blow His disciples out of the water. I want to focus on what was said afterward.

> *John 13:12-17: "When He had finished washing their feet, He put on His clothes and returned to His place. 'Do you understand what I have done for you?' He asked them. 'You call me Teacher and Lord,' and rightly so, for that is what I am. Now that I, your Lord and Teacher, have washed your feet, you also should wash one another's feet. I have set you an example that you should do as I have done for you. I tell you the truth, no servant is greater than his master, nor is a messenger greater than the one who sent him. Now that you know these things, you will be blessed if you do them.'"*

I know the disciples hated it when Jesus started asking questions. Jesus asked them, "Do you understand what I have done for you?" This question was huge for the disciples. Jesus just set the example of how we should live and invest our lives into the lives of people around us.

We must first be willing to submit to God in our spiritual lives. This willingness to submit is the most critical decision we will ever make. The next part of this decision is letting Him control every aspect of your life. That's right, every aspect of our life. I must ask you these questions to get you to stop and think. Does Jesus Christ have total control over your life? Is He Lord over your words, money, thoughts, and friendships? Are you willing to take on the role of a servant for people to see the love of Christ? Does your Friday night lifestyle match your Sunday morning worship? He wants total control of the reins. It seems so hard to turn it all over to Him but look at John 13:17:

**"Now that you know these things, you will be blessed, if you do them."**

What are you waiting for? Why do we run from the One who loves us the most?

*Challenge for today:* Humble yourself before the Lord. Take extra time to worship and praise Him today. Then ask yourself these questions. Have I surrendered control to the Lord over every area of my life? Do people see me as a servant of God? Give God control and hold nothing back from Him today. Pray this: "Lord, I surrender all; I am all in. Amen."

# -11-
# Shake It Off and Step Up

I read an old parable and had to share it with you today. A farmer had an old mule that fell into an abandoned well. The farmer decided that neither the mule nor the well was worth saving, so he got some buddies to help haul dirt to bury the old mule in the well and put him out of his misery. The first shovel of dirt hit the mule on top of the head, and the mule didn't like that one bit. A thought hit the old mule; I'll shake it off and step up. So that's what he did. Shovel after shovel, the old mule fought hard, and he didn't panic and just kept shaking it off and stepping up. Shake it off and step up. Shake it off and step up. Before long, the battered and exhausted mule stepped triumphantly over the wall of the well and into a new chance at life. I love it.

Suppose we refuse to let the regret, bitterness, worry, failures, and guilt that rained down on us bury us? Then those things can lift us to levels we've never reached. Refuse to let these hope killers steal our future and bury us. Shake it off and step up. I want to give you scripture to live by:

*Philippians 4:13: "I can do all things through Christ that gives me strength."*

*2 Timothy 1:7: "For God did not give us a spirit of timidity, but a spirit of power, of love and of self-discipline."*

***Lamentations 3:21-23: "This I call to mind and therefore I have hope. Because of the Lord's great love we are not consumed, for his compassions never fail. They are new every morning; great is your faithfulness."***

I know there are things in this life that can overwhelm us. But don't forget that God loves us. He is for us. It is easy to throw our hands up and roll over in that day-to-day grind, but Satan would win. We cannot allow that to happen. Fight back. Shake it off and step up. Don't buy the lie. Put some truth in your diet.

***Challenge for today:*** When everything seems to be coming down on you and the cares of this world are piling up, turn to the Lord in prayer. Tell Him all about it, but make sure you listen to what He says. Know that God has your best interests in mind and sees you today. He sees your grief, sorrow, worries, and your strife. Our Heavenly Father cares, and He loves you with perfect love. Shake it off and step up. You don't have to face it alone.

# -12-
# Under Pressure

I remember spending time at my grandparents' house when I was young. My grandmothers were always cooking something. If you went to Nanny's house, you were going to eat. I will never forget how she cooked with what I call a pressure cooker. All I knew was that this big pot sat on the stove. It seemed to brew for a long time. When it was done, it would sound off, and Nanny would come running. That pot would hiss at you until you took the pressure off. She was cooking under pressure.

Many of us are living life under pressure. We are overloaded and over-committed. Somehow, we get all tangled up with stress and are pushed to the limit. When that happens, we lose joy, confidence, and friendships and endure life instead of enjoying life. If the Devil can't make you bad, he'll make you busy. Seventy-five percent to ninety percent of all doctor's office visits are from stress-related ailments and complaints. Many of us need a warning sticker on our foreheads that says, "Warning, Content is Under Pressure." We could blow at any moment. Have you ever felt like that? Don't you long for a simple life?

**1 Peter 5:5-7: "Humble yourselves, therefore, under God's mighty hand, that he may lift you up in due time. Cast all your anxiety on him because he cares for you."**

Are you convinced that God cares for you? Until you are convinced, you will never cast your cares on Him. Cast all your cares on the Father and know He cares about you. Sometimes, the best thing to do is stop, take a deep breath or pray. Ask the Lord for wisdom and rest in His grace. He knows what you are going through. Trust Him with it.

*Challenge for today:* Memorize 1 Peter 5:5-7. When the worries of this life come, quote this scripture repeatedly. Know in your heart that He will never leave you or forsake you. Don't try to carry that load because that load is too heavy for you. Get yoked with Christ; He will give you the strength to overcome. Don't allow situations to boil or fester; go to God immediately and ask for help. It will save you a lot of headaches and disappointment.

# -13-
# Use Your Gift

I discovered a short story about a woman shouting at her son, who was hiding under the bed on a Sunday morning. He was crying and refusing to go to their church, which had some problems. "Come out this minute!" the woman shouted. "You are ruining your suit!" "I don't care about my suit." the son said. "You have to go to church." "Tell me one good reason," the son said. "I will tell you three." Because people depend on you, because it honors God, and because you are the pastor!" I hope that isn't your pastor.

> **Romans 12:4-6 says, "Just as each of us has one body with many members, and these members do not have the same function, so in Christ we who are many form one body, and each member belongs to all the others. We have different gifts, according to the grace given us."**

Your talent is God's gift to you. What you do with it is your gift back to God. When we discover that we are called and gifted by God, it changes how we see ourselves, which is so freeing. Nothing is more motivating and encouraging than doing what we are called and created to do. We are a small piece of a vast puzzle. Without you, the picture is not complete. God hasn't gifted anybody to do everything. We need each other. Use your gift. Please share it with the world and overcome the fear. Leave behind the excuses and step out. God has created you for service. It's time to bloom.

Discover your gift, find your place, and glorify God with your talent. You will never possess what you are unwilling to pursue.

*Challenge for today:* Write down what gifts God has given you on paper, then go online and take a spiritual gifts test. Now ask yourself a tricky question. Am I using my gifts for the glory of God? If so, how are you using what God has given you? The Church of Jesus Christ needs everyone to do their part for the glory of the Lord. Step up and be obedient to what God has called you to do. He blesses obedience.

# -14-
# Christ Alone

There are three things I want you to sink your teeth in and chew on.

First, He is more significant than any tradition.

**Colossians 2:8: "See to it that no one takes you captive through hollow and deceptive philosophy, which depends on human traditions and the basic principles of this world rather than Christ."**

Secondly, He is more significant than all your possessions. Now that is stepping on my toes.

**Matthew 13:44: "The kingdom of heaven is like a treasure hidden in the field. When a man found it, he hid it again, and then in his joy went and sold all he had and bought that field."**

The things of this world will not satisfy you and will leave you empty.

Finally, He is greater than the world's transgressions.

**Romans 5:18-19: "Consequently, just as the result of one trespass was condemnation for all men, so also the result of one act of righteousness was justification that brings life for all men. For just as through the disobedience of one man the many**

*were made sinners, so also through the obedience of the one man the many will be made righteous!"*

Christ alone is enough. Nothing needs to be added or taken away. Jesus + 0 = Everything! Because of Jesus, you have been set free from sin and death. Because of His love, you have a plan and a purpose. The tradition and possessions of the world will not satisfy. Christ alone satisfies the soul. I urge you today to seek His face. Take time to soak in His presence and rest there. Let the love of Christ wrap around you. He is enough.

*Challenge for today:* Identify the things in your life that you love. What possessions do you hold dear? How do these things compare to your life of Christ? Know this today, the things of this world will pass away, and they will one day crumble and fall. I encourage you to invest in eternal things that will last forever. It's not wrong to have nice stuff to enjoy, but don't let your love for things outweigh your passion for God. Take time to thank God for His amazing love and grace.

# -15-
# What's In Your Tank?

I drive a 2005 Chevy Colorado truck. It has over 200,000 miles. It gets me from point A to point B and is very dependable. The best thing about it is that it is paid for. It will not be the best ride you have ever had, and you will not be able to roll your windows down, but it will get you where you need to be. One morning, I was headed to work early and noticed I needed to get gas. So, I pulled into the only gas station open at this time of day. I filled up and went on to work. I worked a couple of hours and noticed it was time to grab a quick bite for lunch. I went back out to my truck, turned the key, and it cranked right up just like 100,000 times before. I went to put the transmission in drive, and it died. What happened? I tried it again and again. All it would do is spit, sputter, and then die. What is going on? This problem has never happened before. I had to get the old faithful hauled into a mechanic. He kept her overnight, and he called me the next day. My mechanic asked me, "Who did you tick off?" I responded and said, "Nobody that I know of." He told me that I had water in my gas tank and that he would have to drain everything out of the tank. Then he would have to clean the whole fuel system, but my truck would be fine.

My question is this - what is in your spiritual tank? Is our fuel being watered down? Are we spitting and sputtering when it comes to our walk with Christ? My mechanic had to diagnose my problem and devise a solution fast. He fixed my truck with two easy steps. Don't you love simple things? He emptied all the harmful out and cleaned everything up. Then he added the good clean gas, and my truck was driving like a charm.

> *Colossians 3:5: "Put to death, therefore, whatever belongs to your earthly nature: sexual immorality, impurity, lust, evil desires and greed, which is idolatry."*

> *Colossians 3:8: "Rid yourself of all such things as these: anger, rage, malice, slander, and filthy language from your lip."*

The first step in getting your spiritual engine running again is emptying all the sins and everything that doesn't please God. Everything. You need a time of confession to pour your heart out to Him. Ask Him to cleanse you, heal you, and restore you. The answer is not in adding good gas to the already watered-down tank. You will continue to sputter. Paul goes on to give the second part of the solution.

> *Colossians 3:10 Paul says, "Put on the new self."*

In Christ, the old is gone, and the new has come. Paul also tells us in verse 10, "clothe yourself with compassion, kindness, humility, gentleness, and patience." After your confession, then ask God to fill you.

*Challenge for today:* Ask Him to give you a heart like His and to fill you with joy, passion, humility, and compassion. When it comes down to it, this will be your prayer. Lord, kill me and then fill me. Become a dwelling place that pleases the Lord. I am praying for a smooth-running engine in your life. What's in your tank?

# -16-
# Refocus On the Future

**Philippians 3:13-14: "Forgetting what is behind and straining toward what is ahead, I press on toward the goal to win the prize for which God has called me heavenward in Christ."**

Have you ever stopped to think about why Jesus was so compelling? Why is he considered the most outstanding leader ever to live? Jesus wasn't focused on what people were like. He focused on what they could be. "Thank you, Lord, for your grace and mercy. Thank you, Lord, for not giving up on me or pushing me aside when I messed up in the past. Thank you for seeing the good in me, even when I didn't see it myself." We cannot continue to live our lives looking in the rearview mirror.

I love the story of the woman at the well in John chapter four. She was a lady with a shady past, and yes, she was a Samaritan woman. Why in the world did Jesus stop and talk to her? He knew all about her. We can see that in John 4:16-18, "Jesus told her, 'Go call your husband and come back.' 'I have no husband,' she replied. Jesus said to her, 'you are right when you say you have no husband. The fact is, you have had five husbands, and the man you now have is not your husband.'"

Jesus saw past her mistakes. He saw past her failures and all her shortcomings. He saw the good in her and took the time to invest in her life. The woman at the well ended up sharing with everybody she knew about the love of

31

Christ. Jesus gave her hope for a better future. Fresh vision leads to encouragement. Encouragement leads to hope. Hope leads to change. Change leads to better days.

*Challenge for today:* Don't be so fast to judge others. I am so guilty of this. It is part of our human nature. Give people the benefit of the doubt, and slow down enough to encourage them. That encouragement could change the direction of their lives, touching everyone around them. Let's follow the example of Christ as we walk through today. Focus on what they could be in Christ Jesus.

# -17-
# Raise Your Expectations

In this crazy world that we call life, every single one of us will face discouragement. Discouragement kills our dreams and our passion for life. We must be prepared and ready when it comes our way and realize it is a spiritual attack from Satan himself.

**Matthew 19:26: "With man this is impossible, but with God all things are possible."**

Do you believe that? These words are written in red. These are the very words of Jesus, and you can bank on them. Jesus said it, I believe it, and that settles it. Somehow, many of us have lost the sense of believing in God for the impossible. We settle into life and get stuck in the trap of paying bills and trying our best to get by. Too often, we listen to the negative talk around us and all the naysayers saying, "You can't do that." We shrink back, and we stop trusting God for the miracles. I know; I have walked through that myself. It is time to break those chains, and it is time to change the way we live. We were not created to exist and get by in life. We are made in the image of God, and if we are in Christ, we have the Holy Spirit of God living in us. Yes sir.

Whatever you need, God is greater. Whatever you lack, God will supply. Whenever you are overwhelmed, He will comfort you. He is able. We must raise our expectations of what God can do. Wake up from our slumber. It's time to rise up. More than ever, we must stand on God's Word and not back down. It's time to start believing in God for the impossible.

> **Matthew 13:57-58 "But Jesus said to them, 'Only in his hometown and in his own house is a prophet without honor.' And he did not do many miracles there because of their lack of faith."**

Where is your faith level today?

*Challenge for today:* Have faith in the God of this universe and dream. And when you dream, dream big because we have a huge and mighty God. All things are possible with Him. Today is the day. Wake up, rise up, and believe God for the impossible.

# -18-
# Recharge

Take time now and thank God for another day. Don't take today for granted or look past it. I want to introduce you to a book that will encourage you greatly. The book is called "The Hope Quotient" by Ray Johnston. It is a great read and will be a massive weapon against discouragement.

I want to ask you two questions. The first question is, what fuels you? You must know what motivates you, encourages you, and recharges you. The second question is, what drains you? When I start driving on a trip, I want a full gas tank. The road to a better future is never traveled on an empty tank. Church, we need to fuel up, and let me tell you, we don't need cheap gas. I want to help you identify things that will drain you. Are there unhealthy people in your life, unkind critics, super busy schedules, past guilt, or just an unhealthy environment? Ask the Lord today what you need to change in your life. Ask God to give you wisdom on handling those things that drain you. Don't be afraid to seek godly counsel. One of the best things to do when you are discouraged is to slow down and cry out to God. Staying encouraged requires five supply lines to keep you spiritually and emotionally fueled.

First, invest in your physical, spiritual, and emotional growth. What are you doing this year to get better? What goals have you set for yourself?

Secondly, take time to worship. Worship reconnects you to God and has a way of stoking the fire of hope.

Worship restores your joy. Worship also focuses off of self and puts the spotlight on Jesus Christ.

Third, we need to dive into the Word of God. You will receive strength, power, and godly wisdom from the Word of God. It is vital to push aside that cell phone and take in something that will encourage you. It will fill you with everything you need to live a godly life.

Fourth, surround yourself with people who will make you better. Are there people around you that challenge you to grow? Do you have a mentor that will encourage you and hold you accountable? We all need someone who will cheer us on and get on us when we need it.

Lastly, pay attention to the voices you are listening to. The God of the universe will never leave us nor forsake us. He will give us everything we need to complete our journey.

*Challenge for today:* Identify what fuels you and what drains you. Write these things down and understand what makes you tick. Then worship, not just on Sunday, but daily. It will do your soul good. Please pay attention to what you are taking in, whether it's music, people's opinions, or what you read. Stoke the fire of your soul and guard against getting into a rut spiritually.

# -19-
# The Attack of Discouragement

One of Satan's most effective weapons he uses today is discouragement. Satan knows he is a loser, and he also knows he has lost the war. He wants to cause as much trouble as possible before his final defeat. Discouragement is universal. How will you deal with it when it comes? You may be covered up with dismay right now. The bad news is that once Satan finds a weakness, he will attack repeatedly. Satan fights dirty, and he will do anything to destroy you, your witness, and your family. Discouragement is also contagious. You can catch it from other people. Not only is pessimism contagious, but it is deadly. It will destroy your life, and it will wreck relationships. When we get hit with discouragement, we will get down. The key is not to stay there. God has given us everything we need to fight and win.

> *Second Peter 1:3: "His divine power has given us everything we need for life and godliness through our knowledge of him who called us by his own glory and goodness."*

Don't you know Satan hates that verse? You have a calling to fulfill, you have a job to do, and you have a dream to chase. Don't back down, and don't give up. Keep pressing forward, and do not grow tired of doing good. Several times in my ministry, I felt like I was not reaching the people, but God handed this verse to me.

> *Isaiah 55:11 "So is my word that goes out from my mouth: it will not return to me empty but will accomplish what I desire and achieve the purpose for which I sent it."*

*Challenge for today:* Continue to be faithful and trust that He is still in control. I am not sure what you are facing but know that He loves you and will see you through. Lean on Him and trust Him with all your heart. He sees you where you are today. He knows what it is like to be hit from every side. He is doing mighty works for you as we speak.

# -20-
# Hope

The greatest gift you or I can ever give anyone is hope. If you are in Christ, God calls you a Hope Dealer. We not only receive hope, but we are to give it away. When people lose hope, they lose their ability to dream. Despair replaces joy. Fear replaces faith. Anxiety replaces prayer. Insecurity replaces confidence. When discouragement settles in, parents give up on their kids. Leaders throw in the towel. Healthy emotions are replaced with toxic attitudes, and Satan loves them.

> **Romans 15:13: "May the God of Hope fill you with all joy and peace as you trust in Him, so that you may overflow with hope by the power of the Holy Spirit."**

True hope is only found in a personal relationship with Jesus Christ. The God of hope will not only fill you with joy and peace but also fill you to the point of overflowing with hope. That is a promise written to you. Hope liberates. Hope releases you from your past. It breaks the chains of guilt and past failures. It can free you from bitterness and anger. Hope also motivates. It helps you bounce back. Have you ever noticed how many comeback stories there are in the Bible? Hope looks at the future and not the past. Hope also initiates. Hope sets us free to dream.

*Challenge for today:* Dare to dream today. Don't give up on your dreams. Hope activates. Hope helps us believe that we can make a difference.

**First Corinthians 13:13: "And now these three remain: faith, hope, and love."**

Christianity will never thrive without all three. Today, keep your eyes on the face of Jesus, desire His presence, and place your trust in Him. He will give you everything you need to blaze a trail.

# -21-
# First Thessalonians 3:11-13

This is the day the Lord has made; let us be glad and rejoice in it. Take time to praise Him for the three blessings of life before we get started.

Paul prayed a powerful prayer in First Thessalonians 3:11-13:

*"Now may our God and Father himself and our Lord Jesus clear the way for us to come to you. May the Lord make your love increase and overflow for each other and for everyone else, just as ours does for you. May he strengthen your hearts so that you will be blameless and holy in the presence of our God and Father when our Lord Jesus comes with all the holy ones."*

Paul prayed two things for the early church in these three verses. First, he prayed that their love would increase and overflow for people. Is this something you need in your local body of believers? Do you need a greater flow of love between you and your family? Then pray for it; He hears your prayers. Open your heart and get ready to receive what God has for you. Let His love fills you to the point of overflowing. Let His love spill out everywhere you go.

Then he went on to pray that their hearts would be strengthened to be blameless and holy. This may not seem to be earth-shattering, but this can change your life. I want to ask you to do something. This week, I challenge you to pray this prayer every day and see what God does in your life. I double-dog dare you to do it. I had a pastor named Bobby Harrell who shared wisdom with me many years ago. He said, "Love God and love people. If you can do that, you will do well in ministry."

*Challenge for today:* Lord, wake us up from our selfishness and give us love for other people. We can be so self-centered that we don't see the people around us. Lord, fill us with your love so we can love others. Father, I also pray for a heart that is blameless and holy. Purify my mind and help me to be more like you every day. You must increase, and I must decrease. Simple, but dead on. This is God's Word to us. Will we apply it? Prepare your hearts to be used by God.

# -22-
# Jump

One of my greatest childhood memories happened every weekday around 4:10 pm. My dad would come home from work. My dad was and still is my superhero. I could tell you story after story of the love and sacrifice this man made for our family. My dad worked at the Marine base in Albany, Georgia, and he would get off every day at 4:00. He would take about ten minutes to get home. When he got home, three kids sat on pins and needles, ready to see their dad. As soon as he pulled up to the house, all three of us would take our position at the top of the steps of our home. He would open the car door and run to the bottom of the steps. And one by one, we would jump into his arms. Occasionally, I would forget to wait my turn, and my brother and I would jump simultaneously. Never once did I ever think he would drop me. I trusted him with all my heart. Almost every Friday, each of us would have a special treat in his front pocket. Those were the good ole days.

That is a beautiful picture that will never be erased from my mind. But it's also a word we need to hear in our spiritual lives. Most Christians today live in fear. We fear what other people may think about us or what will happen if we fully obey the Lord. So many of us are standing at the top step and wanting to jump into our Heavenly Father's arms, but fear is holding us back.

***Proverbs 3:5-6:** "Trust in the Lord with all your heart and lean not on your own understanding; in all your ways acknowledge him, and he will direct your paths."*

I don't know what is holding you back from fully trusting the Lord, but He is calling you to take that leap of faith. Come to a point where you fully trust Him and are willing to do whatever He has put in your heart. You may have many excuses for never fully following the Lord, but it is time to jump. You can trust Him. He will catch you every time, and you might be surprised by what He has in His front pocket.

*Challenge for today:* Do you realize how much your Heavenly Father loves you? Then trust Him today. He is standing at the bottom of the steps, waiting for you to jump into His arms. Know this: He will catch you, and it will be the most exhilarating experience in life. Jump.

# -23-
# Psalms 23:5

Have you ever had one of *those* days? My phone died, and my alarm didn't go off at 4:00 am. I was running late and had to rush. Have you ever noticed that is the way life goes? It's how you deal with it when things don't go as planned. How many of us have this grand plan to save money and get ahead? It looks good on paper, but life happens. Next thing you know, the car breaks down, the kids need braces, and the AC unit is on the blink. You know what I am talking about. Let's crack open the Word of God and look at Psalms 23:5:

> **"You prepared a table before me in the presence of my enemies. You anoint my head with oil, my cup overflows."**

God wants to spread a feast of the provision before us in the very presence of our enemies. God doesn't promise to hit the eject button whenever hardships, trials, and challenges surround us. He promises something even more powerful; right amid the trouble, our shepherd spreads a table of provision for us in full view of the things threatening us. Jesus is the Lion of Judah; his voice shatters the enemy.

> **Look what David wrote in Psalms 27:1-3: "The Lord is my light and my salvation-whom shall I fear? The Lord is the stronghold of my life-of whom shall I be afraid? When evil men advance**

*against me to devour my flesh, when my enemies and my foes attack me, they will stumble and fall. Though an army besiege me, my heart will not fear; though war breaks out against me, even then I will be confident."*

David faced life just like anybody else. He probably didn't struggle with paying bills, but he did have his own set of issues when it came to living out life. Through it all, he trusted in the God of heaven.

*Challenge for today:* We decide who sits at our table and who joins that special meal with us. Don't give the enemy a seat at your table. Say no to worry, fear, and doubt. Say no to anxiety and depression today. Place your trust in the very creator of heaven and earth. Know that He loves you, and He has your back. Take your eyes off yourself and the problems of this life and turn them to the presence of God. My cup overflows today.

# -24-
# Pass-Through

Before you read this, please take the time to begin your day in prayer. Take this time to praise Him. Ask Him to forgive you and to cleanse you from sin. Thank Him for the blessings of life. Then, pray over your friends, family, and your needs. Make prayer a priority.

> *Isaiah 43:1b says, "Fear not for I have redeemed you; I have summoned you by name; you are mine."*

If you need some good news today, there it is. I can sit in this chair and say the blood of Jesus Christ has redeemed me. Man, my sins have been forgiven, and I have been made right in the sight of a Holy God. I was dead, but now I am alive. I was blind, but now I see. I was condemned to a place called Hell, but now I am walking in the newness of life. I am His child. I am a child of the living God all because of Jesus.

> *Isaiah 43:2-3: "When you pass through the waters, I will be with you; and when you pass through the rivers, they will not sweep over you. When you walk through the fire, you will not be burned; the flames will not set you ablaze. For I am the Lord your God, the Holy One of Israel, your Savior."*

One thing is sure in life; there will be troubles. Hard times will come. God never said follow me, and you will have a trouble-free life. He said, "When you pass through the waters, when you pass through the rivers, and when you pass through the fire..." Storms will come and go, but one thing is sure. He will be with you every step of the way because He will not leave you or forsake you. He will see you through, so You must trust Him. Can you say today, "I have a Savior, and His name is Jesus?" Are you tired of facing this life alone and trying to do everything with your strength? For many today, you must stop what you are doing and say, "I need you, Jesus." The God of Shadrach, Meshach, and Abednego holds my hand and walks me through life. "Thank you, Lord."

***Challenge for today:*** Make a list of all your worries, concerns, and burdens of life. I am sure it's not just one thing sitting on your shoulders. I encourage you to write them down and look honestly at what is weighing you down. Present this list to the Lord. Spend time talking with your Father and trust Him with it. I pray for your peace and encouragement today. Rest and enjoy God's presence, knowing He cares for you. He is there holding your hand and taking every step with you as you live your life.

# -25-
# Reach Out

Take time today to thank God for what you do for a living. That's right, thank God for your job. I know it can be a hassle, and it is a source of many headaches and complaints. It does supply you with the money you need to eat and pay your bills. Also, thank the Lord for the gift of today, and I pray that you make the most out of every opportunity placed in your path. God's Word is so good.

> *James 5:19-20: "My brothers, if one of you should wander from the truth and someone should bring him back, remember this: whoever turns a sinner from the error of his way will save from death and cover over a multitude of sins."*

> *Galatians 6:1: "Brothers, if someone is caught in a sin, you who are spiritual should restore him gently. But watch yourself, or you may be tempted."*

We all know someone that is struggling in their walk with Christ. At one time or another, we all have been there. We are quick to condemn and judge others or talk about them behind their backs. I encourage you to begin to pray for them. Ask God to open their spiritual eyes and soften their hearts. Before you talk to your friends about God, talk to God about your friends. Then pray that God will allow you to share and love them. Also, pray for wisdom, discernment, and the right words to share with your friend. Let your words be spoken in love and covered in grace. Notice that the scriptures say to restore them gently. They don't need a big Bible upside their head, at least not the oversized coffee table one. Those could hurt!

*Challenge for today:* Who did God just put on your heart? Whose face flashed before you when you read this devotion? Write that person's name down and begin to pray over them. Then be obedient to what God is about to ask you to do. Listen to what God is saying to you because God blesses obedience. You may be tempted to waive this off or even act like you didn't hear what God said to you. Don't walk past this but be willing to be used by God in this person's life. I pray for your courage and faithfulness.

# -26-
# A Sacrifice of Praise

I don't know about you, but I can sometimes be very selfish. Getting caught up in gathering earthly possessions and building my worldly kingdom is easy. We can become so consumed with making a giant nest egg for retirement that we forget to live for today. We chase the dream of owning a colossal home or buying that big fancy truck and all that stuff that could bring us much pleasure. Maybe we want to climb the ladder of success, and we would do anything to get that promotion. When we get to the top of that ladder, we discover that we have climbed the wrong one. The Lord has a message for us today, open your heart and mind to what God wants to show you. Before you move forward and read this devotion, pray, "Father, speak to me and help me to hear from you today. Give me a listening ear and a pure heart." Watch out for distractions; they will trip you up.

> *Hebrews 13:15-16: "Through Jesus, therefore, let us continually offer to God a sacrifice of praise- the fruit of lips that confess his name. And do not forget to do good and to share with others, for which such sacrifices God is pleased."*

> *Jeremiah 33:11: "Give thanks to the Lord Almighty, for the Lord is good; his love endures forever."*

Have you ever been consumed with the worries of life? And when we are consumed with the concerns of this life, we are full of anxiety, fear, and doubt. When Satan hits us with all this, then everything becomes about us. Satan loves to distract us and for us to be consumed with things that don't matter. Life doesn't have to be full of fear and negativity. God wants us to enjoy life and be full of joy. Kick Satan in the mouth and make a sacrifice of praise to the living God. Yes. Take time to worship and praise Him. He is worthy, and it will do us so much good to take the spotlight off ourselves. When we take time to praise and worship, He will show us the needs of other people around us. Spotlights will blind you to the faces in the crowd. That is the truth.

*Challenge for today:* Praise Him and take the spotlight off yourself. See the faces in the crowd, and love on someone today. I urge you to spend extra time thinking of creative ways to encourage people all week. Blow people away with the love of Christ by encouraging them in this crazy world. This pleases God, and it can be a lot of fun.

# -27-
# Is It Clean?

My wife and I had an appointment two years ago to sit and listen to a Rainbow Vacuum Cleaner presentation. I sat through something similar about 20 years ago and bought an expensive vacuum cleaner. I knew what they were going to do in their presentation. They were going to vacuum my carpet and show me how much dirt was in my house. So, I got out my trusty cheap vacuum and went to town. I went over that carpet three times. That carpet was clean. I did all I could to get ready for this presentation. Guess what? After vacuuming three times, they pulled out that Rainbow machine and showed me all the dirt left on my carpet. Are you kidding me? I am not here to sell you a vacuum cleaner, but I want to share something with you.

We can do everything to live a good, moral life. We can feed the homeless, take care of orphans, and give to charity until it hurts. In other words, we can vacuum, vacuum, and vacuum and not get rid of the dirt in our lives. No amount of good work can get rid of all the dirt and sin in our lives.

> **John 3:5, Jesus tells Nicodemus, "I tell you the truth, no one can enter the kingdom of God unless he is born of water and the Spirit."**

It's only through the blood of Jesus Christ that we can be clean. Isaiah 1:18 says, "Though your sins are like scarlet, they shall be white as snow." Sometimes we allow sin to build up in our lives, and we have the attitude that it is no big deal, and before long, it becomes a real big problem. Then we wonder how in the world did I end up here?

> **1 John 1:9: "If we confess our sins, he is faithful and just and will forgive us our sins and purify us from all unrighteousness."**

That is good news. Turn to the one that overcame sin and death. Cry out to the one who loves you because he took your place on the cross. Is your heart clean? Has the blood of Christ washed your heart? What can wash away my sins? Nothing but the blood of Jesus.

*Challenge for today:* Pray, "Lord, cleanse me today. Forgive me when I failed you. Cover me with the blood of Jesus Christ. Wash me whiter than snow. Create in me a clean heart, O God." You can only be genuinely cleaned in the name of Jesus. "Thank you, Lord." The Rainbow vacuum will clean your carpet, but only Jesus can cleanse your heart.

# -28-
# Psalms 141:3

Grab your Bible and turn to Psalms 141:3 and read this verse about five times. That's right, read it five times, and let this word go deep. Let it run where it needs to go. Then ask Him how this can apply to your life today.

**_Psalms 141:3: "Set a guard over my mouth, O Lord; keep watch over the door of my lips."_**

"Lord, open our hearts today so we can hear a clear word from you, and give us understanding and wisdom that only comes from you."

What mental picture does this verse paint for you? How many of us have said things we wish we could take back? One of my favorite toys as a child was a cork gun. It was so much fun to play with, but the best thing about it was that the cork was attached to a string at the end of the gun. I never had to chase it down or stop playing to look for it behind a chair or under the couch. There have been times in my life when I wished I could have had a string on the end of my words. Have you ever been there? You popped off and said something before you thought everything through? It happens to the best of us. Have you ever been to your kid's ball game, and you are so in tune with the game that you feel like you are playing the game yourself? Then the referee, in your opinion, makes a bad call, or a parent on the other team says something about your kid. Then you explode, express yourself, and say what you were thinking to everyone. Then it hits you. Did I say that out loud?

**Proverbs 21:23: "He who guards his mouth, and his tongue keeps himself from calamity."**

The words we speak can tear down, or they can build up. Many of us need to memorize

**Psalms 141:3: "Hide this word in your heart and guard your heart."**

*Challenge for today:* I know what I am about to ask you to do isn't easy, but here it goes. Is there someone in your life you need to go to and say I'm sorry? Think about it. God placed a person in your heart as soon as you read this verse. It is time to swallow your pride and do what you know is right. Make things right with them and with God. Choose to build up, encourage, and find positive words to speak into people's lives. Find one person and encourage them with kind words.

# -29-
# Where is Your Prayer Life?

I have a crazy question to start you out with today. How will tomorrow look if God answers the prayers you prayed for today? I don't know about you, but God has convicted me of my weak prayer life. How often do we sit around the table and repeatedly say the same prayer to check the box? Do we give God our wish list and tell Him goodbye, only to do the same thing tomorrow? How often do we go through the motions of prayer and expect nothing to happen? Or do we pray with doubt dripping from it?

> **Ephesians 1:18-19: "I pray that the eyes of your heart may be enlightened so that you will know the hope to which he has called you, the riches of his glorious inheritance in the saints, and his incomparable power for us who believe. That power is like the working of his mighty strength."**

If you are in Christ, there is a power accompanying your life that is greater than great. God has called us not only to know His Word but also to pray for it. The devil knows that if he can keep our prayer lives silent, he can keep God's hand distant. God has convinced me to go deeper in my prayer life. Pray Heaven down. Lord, make us the prayer warriors you desire. Please help us to stand on your Word and not back down. Give us a heart of compassion for other people and jump-start a powerful prayer life in our hearts.

*Challenge for today:* Take time to evaluate your personal prayer life. Be willing to ask yourself some hard questions and then ask God to show you how you can grow in your prayer journey. Amp up your time in prayer during your time with God, and make prayer a priority in your life. If you are struggling in your prayer life, ask those whom you look up to what they do to break out of a praying rut. Don't worry about changing things or starting a prayer journal. The Father desires to hear from you. Let's pray it up.

# -30-
# Ecclesiastes 3:11

*Ecclesiastes 3:11: "He has made everything beautiful in his time. He has also set eternity in the hearts of men; yet they cannot fathom what God has done from beginning to end."*

He has set eternity in the hearts of men. Grasp that, and do not let go of it. You and I have eternity in our hearts. You have a desire from God that you will never lose, that which will last forever. Anything else is just too small.

We can try to fill our lives with earthly treasures and dreams, but it will leave us empty and unsatisfied. God has made you restless for more because He wants to eternalize your life. We need to make our lives count for something that will last forever. Look at all we are investing in. Things that will one day tear up, break down or be out of date next year. This life is not about your bank account or position at work, and it is not about your retirement plan. How much time do we spend each day on things that will not last? "Lord, give me more, something that matters and will last forever." When my brother-in-law died, it changed my life forever. It opened my eyes, and I will never be the same again. My brother-in-law invested in people. He pointed people to Jesus every day of his life. He invested in the souls of men. God has stirred up a passion in me to make a difference for the rest of my life. It is time to go for it, Church.

*Challenge for today:* Ask God to take your small world and dreams and blow them up. I don't say that in a mean or belittling way. But most of us dream way too small. We serve a huge and mighty God. Your heart has eternity, and you will not be fulfilled until you know you are making an eternal difference. Pray to the Lord and ask Him to shake us up. I challenge you to pray, "Here am I, send me." Invest in things that will last forever.

# -31-
# Wanting More?

Years ago, my wife and I were invited to some friend's house for dinner. We sat down for a meal and began fixing our plates. I had been thinking about this meal all day long. As I surveyed the food, I said, "There has to be more!" Was this all the food prepared for four people? I ate tiny portions and enjoyed our meal with some good friends. When it came time to leave, my stomach was growling like crazy. My wife and I left our friend's house, and I went by the nearest restaurant to grab a couple of hamburgers. I had to have more.

That is the feeling many of us know so well spiritually. We are eating everything that is offered to us spiritually. We go to all the Christian meetings, listen to Christian podcasts, and play all the Christian music we can find, but we are still hungry. We are hungry for something more "filling," more challenging, and powerful. Have you ever said, "I am sick and tired of the status quo?" Maybe your life is full of business, but it's not fulfilling. So often, we pour ourselves into our work and pursue everything under the sun. Still, we are empty. Our "sick and tired of the status quo" is a magnet drawing us toward the greater greatness for which we are created. Our restlessness is a Holy discontentment.

***Deuteronomy 8:3: "He humbled you, causing you to hunger and feeding you with manna, which neither you nor your fathers had known, to teach you that man does not live on bread alone but on***

**_every word that comes from the mouth of the Lord._"**

God made them hungry for the mighty work He would bring into their lives. The people who are spiritually full and satisfied may never taste the manna. There is some excellent news for those who are spiritually restless. Restlessness usually precedes a powerful touch of God in a person's life. God has made you hungry for more, so He can feed you something much bigger.

*Challenge for today:* Identify your holy discontentment. What has God placed in you that you always seem to put off or place on the back burner? It never goes away; it just seems to grow. Do you feel like there is something more to life than what you see on the surface? Are you so caught up in the mundane things of this world that you can't go after your God-dream? Tell God, "I want more." He is listening. What are you waiting for?

# -32-
# Drifting?

I am not much of a beach person these days. I can sit under an umbrella for two hours, and I will get a sunburn. I can feel my skin bubbling. On the other hand, my wife can lay out on a towel all day, and her skin will be golden brown. The beach is not my thing. It hasn't always been like that. I remember, as a child loving to go to the beach. We would have so much fun throwing a ball and building sandcastles. We would take turns covering each other up with sand.

Then we would run to the water and rinse off. We would play out in the water and get lost in everything that was going on. Then we would hear a voice saying, "Stay where we can see you. Don't drift off." Those words went in one ear and out the other ear. We would continue to play and not pay attention to my father's words. It was so easy to get distracted by everything in the water. As a child, you don't think about the danger around you. You don't think about the current and how that can pull you away from the place you are supposed to be. I remember looking up and not seeing my parents. I saw people on the shore, but I didn't recognize them. Where did they go? Have they left us out here by ourselves? We began to look back down the shore, and there they were. They were waving and saying something, but I couldn't hear them. We had drifted away, and we didn't even know it. It was so slow and gradual.

Have you drifted away from the one who loves you the most? Has Satan distracted you and pulled you away

63

from your Father so that you haven't even recognized what is going on? Have you ever been so distracted by what's happening around you that you don't hear your Father's voice? You may be asking yourself, "How did I get here?"

> *Revelation 2:4-5: "Yet I hold this against you; You have forsaken your first love. Remember the height from which you have fallen or ("drifted away from"). Repent and do the things you did at first."*

God is talking, but you are so far away that you can't hear what He is saying. God hasn't left you, but you tend to drift. Look away from the distractions of this world and find your Father. Make your way back to Him. It starts by saying I am sorry; can you forgive me?

*Challenge for today:* Stop long enough to recognize the traps Satan uses on you to pull you away. Identify that weak spot in your armor he always seems to aim for. Admit your weaknesses but have a plan in place to strengthen what is weak. Make sure you have other people around to encourage you and hold you accountable. Stay grounded and rooted in God's Word. It will keep your eyes focused on the Father.

# -33-
# Psalms 139:1-4

There is nothing like an early morning with a cup of coffee and the Word opened in Psalms. Psalms 139:1-4:

*"O Lord, you searched me and you know me. You know me when I sit and when I rise; you perceive my thoughts from afar. You discern my going out and my lying down; you are familiar with all my ways. Before a word is on my tongue you know it completely, O Lord."*

No one knows me like God. Even when we don't sense His presence, He is always watching and working behind the scenes. He is always guiding us to Himself.

*Psalms 121:1-4: "I will lift up my eyes to the mountains; from whence shall my help come? My help comes from the Lord, who made heaven and earth. He will not allow my foot to slip; He who keeps you will not slumber. Indeed, he who watches over Israel will never slumber or sleep."*

What a comfort to know that I am never alone, and He is with me everywhere I go. It is remarkable that He loves me so much that He watches my every move. What an amazing God I serve. Amen.

I lived out in the middle of the country, away from civilization. Cotton fields surround my house, and huge deer walk around in herds. Even though I am in the country, I still set my ADT alarm at night. It's my security when I close my eyes to sleep. That alarm guards my house, my belongings, and my family. It blows me away to even think about how much God loves me. He guards His children night and day. The watchfulness of God is something that our minds can hardly grasp. To be kept by God is to be protected under His control and secured as His possession. "Lord, help me today to understand how much you care. Please help me not lose sight of your presence in my daily life. Thank you for your guiding hand and your directions every day."

*Challenge for today:* I know this is a crazy challenge, but I think it will be worth your trouble. Set the alarm on your phone at the top of every hour. Stop what you are doing when that alarm goes off and say, "I am loved and adored by God, and He is right here with me." Practice His presence and know that you are never alone. He is with you 24 hours a day.

# -34-
# Praise To God Who Delivers

David understood the stronghold of God well. David was a servant of God with many enemies and was pursued by Saul's hand. David lived a life full of stress and anxiety. Yet David was able to sing this song to the Lord.

> **Psalm 18:1-2: "I love you, O Lord, my strength. The Lord is my rock, my fortress, and my deliverer; my God is my rock, in whom I take refuge. He is my shield and the horn of my salvation, my stronghold."**

David had a living God that he could trust. When life was falling apart, he ran to the One who held it all together. It was here, in the fortress of God, that David found his shelter. How can we find that spiritual place? We begin by loving Jesus.

> **John 14:21: "Whoever has my commands and obeys them, he is the one who loves me. He who loves me will be loved by my Father, and I too will love him and show myself to him."**

If we follow Christ in love and obedience, He will continue to reveal himself to us. God has so much to show us about Himself. What are you facing today that seems to be too much to handle? It could be debt, a wayward child, a broken relationship, or even sickness. I understand, and I think we have all been there. Sometimes we want to throw our hands up and roll over. All this stress and hassle can be draining, affecting your health. When life is falling apart, there is a place you can find rest and protection. It's located in the presence of a loving God. Lord, bring us to your lap. Hold us to Your heart and assure us of Your Spirit's fullness. "Praise you, Lord."

*Challenge for today:* Commit Psalm 18:2 to memory and quote this verse out loud when the pressures of this life stack up. Say it repeatedly until you believe it. Know in your heart that He is your rock, fortress, and deliverer. You can trust Him, and you can lean on Him when you seem to be overwhelmed. Praise Him for His faithfulness.

# -35-
# Reborn

What does it mean to be born again? I know this is a term I have heard my whole life growing up in the church. It's not just a remodeling job performed by us. Think about the millions of dollars spent yearly on gym memberships, makeup, and beauty products. People hope to reshape their faces or bodies, while others seek inner peace and renewal through drugs or alcohol. Man cannot renew himself. The truth is that God created us, and only God can recreate us. Only God can give us the new birth we desperately want and need.

> **John 3:16: "For God so loved the world, that He gave His only begotten Son, that whoever believes in Him should not perish, but have everlasting life."**

My life has been changed forever because of what Christ did for me on the cross. I have been made new. I am a new creation because of the cross and the empty tomb. I have been forgiven and welcomed into the family of God and given new hope. I will spend all my days forever and ever worshiping the King of kings. Amen. This new birth is the beginning of a new life path under His control. Lives can be remarkably changed, marriages restored, and neighborhoods improved because of the saving grace of Jesus Christ. Perhaps you have been searching your whole life to fill a void in your heart and a purpose for living. You have been trying to fill that void with success, money, or power, but nothing seems to work. It has not brought you peace or happiness. Man, apart from God, is spiritually dead. He needs to be born again. We need to be reconstructed and made new by the blood of Jesus Christ. This new birth can only occur through God's grace and faith in Christ.

*Challenge for today:* If you were to die and come face to face with Jesus, would He welcome you into heaven? I pray that you have a personal relationship with Jesus. I pray that there is no doubt about where you stand in Christ. Have you answered that knock at your heart's door? Receive His love, grace, and His mercy. It will be the greatest decision you will ever make. Have a great day, and tell someone about what Christ has done in your life.

# -36-
# Man's Cry

As a father, I raised two beautiful girls. I think back to when I could hold them in my arms. I remember those days like it was yesterday. These two independent solid ladies depended on me for their every need when they were infants. When they cried, I was there to change their diapers or give them a bottle.

Our heavenly Father does the same for us. Man has two significant spiritual needs. The first is forgiveness. God heard that cry for forgiveness and answered it at Calvary. God sent His only Son to this world to die for our sins so we can be forgiven. This is God's gift to us, God's gift of salvation. It is for everyone who reaches out and accepts the sacrifice of Jesus Christ. "Thank you, Lord."

God also hears our second cry, the cry of goodness. He answered that at Pentecost. God doesn't want us to come to Christ by faith and live a life of defeat and discouragement. Instead, God wanted to fulfill every desire for goodness and the work of faith with power so that the name of the Lord Jesus may be glorified in you. God added the gift of the Holy Spirit to the gift of forgiveness. He gives us the power to be truly good. If you believe in Jesus Christ, power is available to you that can change your life, your marriage, and your relationships. God offers power that can change a tired church into a vital church. I want to thank God for the gift of salvation and the promise of the Holy Spirit. He has given us everything we need to live a life that honors Him.

*Challenge for today:* Celebrate the gift of salvation. Be creative in your celebration; bake a cake and put candles on it. Do whatever it takes to tell the Lord, "Thank you." Thank Him for the gift of His Son, Jesus. Don't take this gift for granted. Offer up sacrifices of praise to your Heavenly Father. But don't stop there; thank Him for the gift of the Holy Spirit. He has given us everything we need to live out our Christian faith. Christ in you, the hope of all glory, lives inside you.

# -37-
# The Stone Was Rolled Away

*Matthew 28:2-6: "There was a violent earthquake, for an angel of the Lord came down from heaven and, going to the tomb, rolled back the stone and sat on it. His appearance was like lightning, and his clothes were white as snow. The guards were so afraid that they shook and became dead men. The angel said to the women, 'Do not be afraid, for I know that you are looking for Jesus, who was crucified. He is not here; he has risen, just as he said!'"*

Therefore, we celebrate Easter. Our God is not dead, and He is alive and well! He has overcome sin, the cross, and death. He has won the victory. Can you imagine this from Satan's point of view? He thought he had the victory in hand, and they were partying with a grand celebration. But the stone was rolled away. That is when the party stopped in Hell. Satan knew he had been defeated. You see, the stone was not rolled away to let Jesus out; the stone was rolled away to let the world see what God had done. Grace moved the stone for you and me. Jesus willingly laid down his life to die a cruel death on a wooden cross. He went through pain and humiliation because of His love for us. At any moment, He could have called ten thousand angels and struck everybody dead that put him on that cross. He knew what He had to do.

I praise God for my risen Savior. Because of what Jesus has done for me, I can celebrate today. Because He lives, I can face tomorrow. Because He lives, all fear is gone. Because He lives, I have eternal life, and one day I will be able to spend eternity with God the Father, praising Him forever and ever. How about you? Do you have a personal relationship with the risen Savior? Have you ever fallen on your knees before God and said you are sorry? Have you ever asked Him to forgive you?

*1 John 1:9: "If we confess our sins, he is faithful and just and will forgive our sins and purify us from all righteousness."*

This is the good news. Today is the day of salvation.

*Romans 10:9: "That if you confess with your mouth, 'Jesus is Lord,' and believe in your heart that God raised him from the dead, you will be saved."*

*Challenge for today:* Paint this picture in your mind. Jesus is standing at your heart's door, knocking. Will you answer His call? It will be the greatest decision you will ever make. He did all the work; all you must do is receive His amazing love. Open the door. Thank God that the stone was rolled away. Rejoice and celebrate our risen King's victory over sin and death. "Thank you, Lord, for your grace and mercy." Share your story with someone who needs to hear the Good News.

# -38-
# Where Can I Find God?

A drunkard was looking for something on the sidewalk one night under a streetlight. He searched along the ground, felt the cement, and occasionally grabbed the pole for support. A person passing by asked what he was looking for. "I lost my wallet," the drunken man replied. The gentleman offered to help him look but with no success. "Are you sure you lost it here?" He asked the man. "No, I didn't." the drunk replied. "It was a half a block back there." "Then why aren't you looking for it back there?" "Because answered the drunken man with baffling logic, "there aren't no streetlights back there."

Searching is essential, but it only works if we search in the right places. We often try to figure out life and find answers to our questions, but we seem to be looking in the wrong places. Are you looking for a purpose, someone to spend your life with, a way to handle pain, or to answer tough questions? We must look in the right place. It all begins and ends in the One we call Jesus. Start there.

As I was reading this week, I came across an old book called, "The Stronghold of God by Francis Frangipane." If you have never read it, you need to order it today. We all go through a time of desolation in our walk with Christ. We enter a spiritual desert when we don't hear the voice of God, and our motivation to serve Him is shallow. Be encouraged today. The truth is that God will use this time of desolation to prepare for a new beginning of power and service. Our task is to be still and know he is God. Check out this prayer and pray this out to God. "Lord, how easily I fall into dead religious habits and spiritual dullness. Lord, I long to know your ways, to have eyes that see and ears that hear. Teach me the intimacies of God. Remove the mystery surrounding yourself that I might truly know you. Forgive me for looking for signs instead of listening to your voice. O God, how I long to truly know You as Moses did and to abide in Your glory. Restore to Your Church the double portion You have promised and guide us into the fullness of your power. Amen."

*Challenge for today:* Make sure to look in the right place when looking for answers to difficult questions. Go to the One in control who cares more for you than anybody. Run to the Father, seek His presence, and rest in His arms. Don't be in a hurry but enjoy His embrace. Spend extra time soaking in His Word, and let it go deep.

# -39-
# Return to the Fortress

I love that old saying, "If the devil can't make you bad, he will make you busy." How accurate is that statement? Satan uses that philosophy on many good-hearted Christian people. We are all guilty at some time or another of being so busy with good stuff that we don't get to enjoy the best stuff. If the enemy can distract us from our time alone with God, he will keep us isolated from the power and help that comes from God to overcome our battles. We sincerely strive to accomplish God's will, but sometimes we forget something significant, the companionship of Jesus. Often, we become so consumed with our battles that we are no longer aware of the presence of Jesus. We are trying to accomplish His will in our strength. It will not take long for the devil to pounce on us.

We must understand that yesterday's anointing is insufficient for today's battle. Just as my body needs constant nutrition and fuel to keep growing and to remain healthy, our soul works the same way. We need a continental dose of Jesus daily to keep going and stay healthy spiritually.

> *Zechariah 9:11-12: "As for you also, because of the blood of My covenant with you, I have set your prisoners free from the waterless pit. Return to your fortress, O prisoners of hope; even now I announce that I will restore twice as much to you."*

Return to the stronghold of God, which comes from fellowship with Christ. We must make our time alone with God our highest priority and not allow Satan to distract us from it. No excuses.

*Challenge for today:* Return to your fortress. God has provided spiritual protection for his children, a stronghold where our souls can always find a safe harbor. You can rest there. Keep the main thing, the main thing.

# -40-
# Are You in The Wrong Place?

David was called "A man after God's own heart." He was Israel's appointed king, wrote great love songs to God, and was a mighty warrior. David seemed to have it all. What happened? Where did everything begin to change?

*Second Samuel 11:1: "In the spring, at the time when kings go off to war, David sent Joab out with the king's men and the whole Israelite army. But David remained in Jerusalem."*

It all started with David being somewhere he wasn't supposed to be. He was the king and should have been with his army at war. Instead, he fell to temptation and sinned against God and his fellow man. Like most of us, we will try and cover it up when we fail. Then everything becomes worse and worse. It's just a matter of time before sin finds you out. It will cost you more than you ever wanted to pay.

In Second Samuel 12, the Lord sent Nathan to confront David about his sin. David had to face his sins, which hit him like a ton of bricks.

*As a result of this sin, David wrote Psalm 51:1-3: "Have mercy on me, O God, according to your unfailing love; according to your great compassion, blot out my transgressions. Wash away all my iniquity and cleanse me from my sin.*

*For I know my transgressions and my sin is always before me."*

*David didn't stop there. He said in verses 10-12, "Create in me a clean heart, O God, and renew a steadfast spirit within me. Do not cast me from your presence or take your Holy Spirit from me. Restore to me the joy of your salvation."*

Are you in the wrong place? Are you running from God and his call for your life? You know you are not living the life that is pleasing to God. You are miserable, but you don't know how to stop it. I encourage you to pray this prayer David prayed to God.

*Challenge for today:* Ask Him to forgive you, cleanse you, and restore that joy that you once had. Come to the place where you can be repaired and renewed. That place is in the arms of your Savior.

# -41-
# Psalms 34:17-19

Cutting grass in Southwest Georgia in the middle of summer can be brutal. It can be close to 100 degrees, and humidity can be off the charts with no wind to cool things down. After a couple of hours of hard work, all you want to do is to be refreshed and cooled down. Your clothes will be covered with sweat, and your body will be drained. The best thing to do is to sit still for a few moments, find a shade tree, down some ice-cold water, and get refreshed. I want you to sit and be restored today. I am inviting you to enjoy the waterfall of His love. What a privilege we have to soak in the presence of the living God. Dive into His Word and take in the very words of the Lord.

*Psalms 34:17-19: "The righteous cry out, and the Lord hears them; he delivers them from all their troubles. The Lord is close to the broken-hearted and saves those who are crushed in spirit."*

Just a simple word this morning, HE HEARS YOU. He understands your pain and precisely what you are going through. Hang on to the promise and know that He will deliver you.

*Psalms 34:8: "Taste and see that the Lord is good; blessed is the man who takes refuge in him."*

*Challenge for today:* Run to the One who loves you the most. Allow the Father to love on you today and rest there. Don't be in a hurry to rush off. I pray for your comfort, peace, and joy. He hears you. Rest in His presence.

# -42-
# Grab His Hand

***Psalms 119:105: "Your Word is a lamp to my feet and a light for my path."***

Lord, shine on our path today, and we will praise you. This world is dark, but the Lord will guide us through it all if we trust Him to direct us. Don't be overwhelmed by the darkness and confusion; focus on the light of Christ. How many of us need this encouragement? God's Word is rich with truth and wisdom that can inspire, motivate, and encourage us.

Please read the entire passage of Matthew 14:22-32. The story of Peter walking on water is rich and filled with truths we can apply to our lives. We all know the story of Peter getting out of the boat and walking to Jesus. But in Matthew 14:30, he became fearful when he saw the wind. Can you relate to that? As a result of seeing the wind and giving in fear, Peter began to sink into the water. As soon as Peter asked for help, Jesus was there. He reached out his hand to pull Peter up out of the water.

***Matthew 14:31 Jesus said to Peter, "You of little faith, why did you doubt?"***

In no way was Jesus being critical. Notice that this comment to Peter was said when they were alone in the water. Then they climbed into the boat. Jesus gently helped Peter locate the source of his problem. For the first time in his life, Peter understood his dependence on faith much more deeply than he would have if he had never left the boat. It was his willingness to risk failure that helped him to grow.

I hate to fail, and I surely do not want to fall in front of others. The reality of life will slap us in the face and never apologize. We are all going to fail sooner or later in life. I don't care who you are. But failure does not shape you; how you respond to failure shapes you. Jesus is whispering to you that it is ok. He makes it clear what you will need to do to grow. Yes, you have fallen, but NOW it's time to get up. Let's get back in the boat, and let's get going. Peter sank into the water, but that didn't define him. Peter made a difference in this world, and we are still reading about him centuries later. Grab Jesus by the hand and continue the journey God has mapped out for you.

*Challenge for today:* Identify your fears. What stops you from going all in with Christ? I challenge you to face those fears head-on and not back down. If you are like most of us, you have met failure and disappointment along the way. That is okay. Get back up and keep your eyes on Christ. Come to a point where you depend on Him and watch how God will grow you. Don't give up, don't back down, and trust that He will light your path.

# -43-
# Where Is Your Focus?

I encourage you to reread Matthew 14:22-33 today; repetition aids learning. Place yourself in that boat with Peter and the other disciples on that crazy day. Imagine what it would be like to live out this scripture and experience the conversations and reactions to what is about to take place. This would be one of those things you would never forget, and it would be a miracle that would shape the rest of your life.

After a long day of ministering to a large group of people, in Matthew 14:22-24, Jesus didn't ask his disciples to lay down and take a nap, but he commanded them to get into a boat and go ahead of him to the other side while he dismissed the crowd. Then Jesus went up to the mountainside to pray. When evening came, the disciples were far from the land, and the wind began to pick up and caused the waves to slam against the boat. In verse 25, Jesus went out to them, walking on water. Have you ever had one of *those* days? The disciples were exhausted by ministering to so many people. Then Jesus commanded them to row across a vast body of water. Then they got caught up in a storm, and a ghost was walking across the lake. It was coming right at them. Of course, Peter couldn't just sit back and listen to what Jesus had to teach them.

**Matthew 14:27-28 Jesus says, "Take courage! It is I. Don't be afraid." Peter said to Jesus: "Tell me to come to you on the water."**

Can you see the faces of the other disciples when Peter spoke those words? Then Jesus told Peter to come to Him on the water. I am sure Peter's heart was pounding fast, and overwhelmed with fear. But Peter's eyes were centered on Jesus. He was locking his eyes on the Savior of the world. He overcame his fear and walked toward Jesus. Can you imagine the courage it took to put one foot over the side of that boat? I know I would have had a death grip on the side of that boat. But he let it go. He abandoned himself utterly to the power of Jesus. I can imagine Peter was beaming with delight, and I believe Jesus was thrilled with his student. Then it happened. In verse 30, Peter "saw the wind." Reality set in. Peter had to be thinking, what was I thinking? Have you ever been there? The wind should have come as no surprise-it had been there all along.

What took place is that Peter's focus shifted from the Savior to the storm. Maybe you are trying to serve God in a new role or to live for him. In the beginning, you are full of faith, and everything is going well. Then reality sets in. Life happens; setbacks, unexpected obstacles, and even hard times. You see the wind. This world is a very stormy place. I don't want to oversimplify this but keep your focus on Christ. Obstacles are to be expected. Where is your focus? On the storm? Or on Christ?

*Challenge for today:* Turn your eyes to Jesus; walk away from your fears and worries. Place your trust in the One who can calm the storms of life, then step out on faith in doing what God has called you to do. Let go of that death grip you have on possession and power. Take that first step and know He is right there with you. Where is your focus?

# -44-
# The Process

Buster Posey is a Major League catcher for the San Francisco Giants. He has three World Series rings and was named Rookie of the Year and MVP. Posey is a very respected leader throughout the league. He is from my hometown right here in Leesburg, Georgia. Many of us had the privilege to watch him grow up playing Little League baseball. Everybody knew he had something special, but greatness didn't happen overnight, and he was never perfect. He did strike out, his arm got sore, and injuries came along, but he kept pushing through. He kept his eye on the prize. Making it to the Major Leagues is a considerable accomplishment; being an All-Star and one of the best is almost impossible. It took blood, sweat, and tears. It was a process, and he was willing to walk it out.

There is a consistent pattern in God's Word of what happens in a life when God wants to use you or grow you. We can see it repeatedly in scripture. There is always a call. God loves to use original people to do extraordinary things. With that call, there will always be fear. Answering God's call can be overwhelming. Even Moses made every excuse in the book because of his fear. But there will always be reassurance. He will never leave us or forsake us. He puts the right people, with the right words, at just the right time to encourage us. He will send His peace to comfort us. Then you will always need to decide. Yes, or no? Will I follow with faithful obedience, or will I walk away? We will have to decide. Finally, there is always a change. Even when you say yes, you will not always walk perfectly. Because of your yes, He will grow you even in your failures. Those who say no will also change. They become a little harder and a little more resistant to the work of God.

*Challenge for today:* Answer these questions. What is God putting in front of you? What is He calling you to do? One thing is certain regarding a relationship with Christ; He doesn't want us to sit still. He wants to see growth in our lives, and He wants us to answer the call. It's time for the Church to overcome our fears and come to a place of obedience. It will not always be easy, but it will be worth it. Where are you in this process?

# -45-
# Jeremiah 33:1-3

Have you ever tried to figure God out? Have you ever wondered why God allows certain things to come our way? Do you ever question if God really cares about you and what goes on in your life? Why do good people have to face difficult times in their lives? Why do faithful men and women of God seem to have it the hardest and face more trials than the guy who cares nothing about God? I am not the only one who has ever asked God difficult questions.

> *Jeremiah 33:1-3: "While Jeremiah was still confined in the courtyard of the guard, the Word of the Lord came to him a second time. This is what the Lord says, he who made the earth, the Lord who formed it and established it- the Lord is his name. Call me and I will answer you and tell you great and unsearchable things you do not know."*

I don't know about you, but I needed to hear this word. I love the way the Lord moves and works in each one of our lives. I don't always understand His timing, but I see how much He cares for me. Jeremiah was in a tough spot. He was confined in jail. I don't know what is going on in your life or what trials you may face, but I know that we all will have storms in our lives sooner or later. The truth is that the word of God can reach you no matter where you are.

*Challenge for today:* I urge you to call upon the Lord. How long has it been since you sat down with the Father of all creation? Is there something you need to get straight with God that you've been trying to avoid for some time? Swallow your pride and stop listening to the enemy's lies. God desires fellowship with you and wants to tell you so many things. Now is the time. You are not to wait for tomorrow or next month. Stop what you are doing and call on Him. He will answer, but don't be surprised by what He tells you. He is a good Father.

# -46-
# 1 Peter 5:6-7

We all face different seasons in life. There are times of great joy and happiness that come our way. There are seasons of learning and growth that help us mature and thrive. There are also times when we face difficulties, struggles, and heartache. Maybe you woke up this morning with something on your mind that has weighed you down for some time, and you can't stop worrying about it. You have tried your best to shake it or let it go, but nothing seems to help. You have tried everything possible to deal with this situation, hurt, or this troubled relationship. You can't get it off your mind; if you were honest with yourself, it is wearing you out. Carrying this weight has caused health issues, stress, and even depression. You have tried your best to cope with it, but it only seems to grow.

I want you to try something. Go to a quiet place. Make sure you are all alone with no distractions. Make sure you leave that cell phone behind in another room. Sing your favorite worship song and sit there and listen to the voice of your Father. Take a second to rest in your Father's arms.

*Open your Bible and turn to First Peter 5:6-7: "Humble yourselves, therefore, under God's mighty hand, that He May lift you up in due time. Cast all your anxiety on Him because He cares for you."*

Now, I want you to tell the Lord what is bothering you. Lay it all out there for Him. Humble yourself under the mighty hand of God and surrender control. Are you convinced that God cares for you? Until you are convinced, you will never cast your cares on Him. Trust Him with it and leave it there with Him.

***Challenge for today:*** Memorize First Peter 5:6-7 and hide it in your heart. Repeat this verse repeatedly, especially on those difficult days. Tell Him that you trust Him and repeat that prayer throughout the day. When anxiety and worry begin to build up, say, "I trust you, Lord." Our God has big shoulders. Cast all your cares on Him. We are trying to carry a load that will eventually wear us out. He cares for you. Lighten your load. He can make our journey a lot more enjoyable.

# -47-
# Have You Ever Heard This Voice?

***Let's look at Luke 4:1-3: "Jesus, full of the Holy Spirit, returned from Jordan and was led by the Spirit in the desert, where for forty days he was tempted by the devil. He ate nothing during those days, and at the end of them he was hungry. The devil said to him, 'If you are the Son of God, tell this stone to become bread.'"***

There is so much in those three verses, but I want to focus on these few words, "The devil said." Have you ever heard that voice? That's the voice that always says, "Who are you?" You can't do that. You don't have what it takes. You are so ugly, and everybody hates you." The sad part about it is that so often, we believe lies. We listen to the wrong voice and turn a deaf ear to the voice of our Heavenly Father. For years I have shrunk back and listened to that voice that said, "Who are you? You are just a boy from the East side of town. You don't have the proper education and will never make a difference."

I heard a message this past weekend about these verses in Luke, which has changed me forever. Jesus had a call to come to earth and give His life on the cross. He said "Yes"¹ to God and to the mission that He was called to do. Because of his "Yes" to God, Jesus could say "NO" to the devil. Because of His "Yes," I can experience life and life more abundantly. I have a calling to teach and preach the Word of God. I am saying "Yes" and choosing to listen to the words of my Heavenly Father. I am a child of the King. I have the Holy Spirit living inside of me. I am anointed by God to share His Word and to encourage His church. What about you? What has God put in your heart? What is your calling and purpose in life? Have you been listening to the wrong voice?

*Challenge for today:* "The devil said." Say no to that voice and yes to Jesus and his calling on your life. It's time to walk in victory and believe the truth instead of lies. We can't shrink back and dream small dreams. Press forward, and don't look back. Rise up and listen to the voice of your Heavenly Father.

# -48-
# Willingness To Look Foolish

Every one of us has dreams, but very few run after them. As a young boy, I dreamed of becoming a professional baseball player. I was pretty good and thought I had a shot at making it. I was twenty years old, married, and working at the local cable company. I wasn't making much money, but it was a steady job. We owned a cute little house, and we were comfortable. That dream of playing professional ball was stronger than ever. If I don't go for it, would I be content not trying? How could I do that now with all these new responsibilities as a husband and provider? I went for it. I quit my job, sold my house, and moved in with my sister-in-law to train for my shot at playing professional baseball. What would people say? How foolish will I look to people if this doesn't work out?

All these questions ran through my mind, but I decided to go for it, even though I may look foolish. I trained and prepared to get ready for several different tryouts, but MLB just happened to have a strike that year. No, I didn't make it; that year, baseball shut down, and I had to go back home to find a real job. I may have looked foolish, but I went for it. No regrets.

Sometimes faith is the willingness to look foolish. How about Noah building an ark in the middle of a desert? I bet Moses looked silly asking Pharaoh to let his slaves go. The Israelite Army had to look foolish marching around Jericho, yelling and blowing a trumpet. What about that little boy going to fight an armed giant with a slingshot? I think that wasn't very smart. How about that guy called Peter? How stupid was it for him to get out of a perfect boat in the middle of a lake to try and walk on water to Jesus? The results speak for themselves. Noah built that boat, it floated, and it saved his family. Pharaoh let the children of Israel go, and God worked many crazy miracles on their journey to their new home. The Israelite army marched around Jericho, raising cane, and the walls tumbled down. How crazy is that? We all know how the story of David and Goliath went. The big boy fell at the feet of a shepherd boy because of his willingness to look foolish. Peter did something that no one else had ever done except Jesus. He walked on water. If we aren't willing to look stupid, we are foolish. Many people have never built an ark, become a national leader, killed a giant, experienced a great victory, or walked on water.

*Challenge for today:* Identify your God-dream. What has God put in your heart? Don't be scared to step out on faith and do what He calls you to do. He blesses obedience.

# -49-
# Resisting God's Call?

Before our devotion for today, ask the Lord to open your spiritual eyes and ears. Right now, ask Him to enlighten your heart to discover the calling of God in your life. Then pray that you can receive the vision and the words He has for you today.

> **Jonah 1:1-2: "The word of the Lord came to Jonah son of Amittai: Go to the great city of Nineveh and preach against it, because its wickedness has come up before me."**

This was a call from God straight to Jonah, but Jonah didn't want anything to do with it. Look what happens in the following verse of Jonah 1:3: "But Jonah ran away from the Lord and headed to Tarshish. He went down to Joppa, where he found a ship bound for that port. After paying the fare, he sailed for Tarshish to flee from the Lord."

Can you relate to Jonah today? After Jonah ran from God, nothing went right until he obeyed what God called him to do.

Often, when God called people into His service, they resisted by coming up with many excuses. This practice of resistance was true even of the strongest and best leaders in the Bible. Moses led the group for multiple reasons. Moses said in Exodus 4, "Who am I? No one will listen to me. I am not even a speaker. Lord, send someone else."

*Gideon, in Judges 6:15, said: "I am nobody. I am the weakest in my family."*

*Solomon in 1 Kings 3:7: "I am only a child." Jonah said nothing and ran away.*

In contrast, see the responses of Isaiah and Mary. When Isaiah was called, he replied, "Here am I, send me." (Isaiah 6:8). Mary said, "I am the Lord's servant. May it be to me as you have said." (Luke 1:38). We can come up with several excuses not to follow the calling of God. I have used a couple of good ones myself over the years. When God puts something on your heart, don't push it aside and pretend it's no big deal. Follow your heart and be willing to be obedient to what God has placed before you.

*Challenge for today:* Take time to build an altar and turn your focus to the One calling you. Today is when you stop resisting the Lord's call on your life. Stop running and tell Him, "I surrender all." Let the peace flow. Think about this; It took Jonah a lot longer to obey God than it did for a whole city to be saved. What are you waiting on? Answer the call.

# -50-
# Question

I want to ask you a question because I want to give you something to think about. What is your passion? I am not asking about your desires or what you like to do because our desires change daily. Ask yourself, what breaks your heart? What is your holy discontent? What has God put in you for a reason and a purpose? I believe God has given every believer a calling and a purpose in this life. Yes, He has also allowed us to use our gifting and our passion for His glory. But have you ever noticed that God's opportunities are usually wrapped up in obstacles? In other words, it will require faith and a willingness to trust your Heavenly Father.

Many of us are waiting on some great faith to act on it, but all God asks is to have the faith of a mustard seed. Jesus was teaching and told this parable in Matthew 13:31-32:

*"The kingdom of heaven is like a mustard seed, which a man took and planted in the field. Though it is the smallest of all your seeds, yet when it grows, it is the largest of garden plants and it becomes a tree so that the birds of the air come and perch in its branches."*

God loves to take our small dreams and passions and turn them into God-sized realities.

*Challenge for today:* Find out your passion and purpose for this life. Pray daily and ask God to make that clear to you. Then grow in it. Have you ever noticed that your workouts are always shorter when you work out alone? Find a mentor—someone who will challenge you and encourage you. God's opportunities are always bigger than yours. Fear will be waiting around the corner. All you will need is a hint of faith. Follow your passion and seek God with all your heart.

# -51-
# A Father's Desire

Being a father is one of a man's greatest privileges. God blessed me with two beautiful girls. I remember the days before they were born, and I wondered what they would look like. Would they have my big teeth? I remember praying over them months before they were ever born. I still remember that prayer even to this day, some 27 years later. As the years have passed and time has flown by. They have grown up before my eyes. They are two beautiful women that have blessed my life. Where does the time go? It has been a journey. Don't get me wrong; there have been some difficult times. It wasn't always easy, but we shared many great memories. We were held together by a constant love for each other and God Himself.

As a father, I love to spend time with my girls. Whether it's going to the gym, watching a movie, or watching them play soccer. But what I enjoy the most is sitting down and hearing their hearts and for them to share their passions and struggles with me. I want to be a big part of their lives. I want to do all I can to help them, encourage, and equip them to be the woman God has called them to be. That's a father's desire. I love it when they call and ask if I have time to get a cup of coffee and talk. It hit me; that is my Heavenly Father's greatest desire too. To spend time with His children and hear our desires, passions, and struggles. I am unsure how I would handle it if my girls didn't come to me and share their life. It could break my heart.

**Psalm 116:1-2: "I love the Lord, for he heard my voice; he heard my cry for mercy. Because he turned his ear to me, I will call on him as long as I live."**

Call out to Him today.

*Challenge for today:* Slow down. Clear your schedule and make time for the very Creator of heaven and earth. Enjoy sitting in the presence of greatness and enjoy His company. Your Heavenly Father is waiting for you. Make the time, and it will be so worth it. Make God smile because He loves spending time with you. That is His greatest desire.

# -52-
# Hope

I have a favorite t-shirt that I wear all the time. My wife thinks it is the only shirt I have in my closet. On the front of this shirt it has two words written across the front. "Hope Dealer" I love seeing people's expressions and responses. It does open the door for great conversation. We, as Christian believers, need to share our hope in Jesus Christ. We don't need to keep it inside the four walls of a building or locked inside us. God hasn't given us the spirit of fear but of power. There is a world out there that needs to hear the Good News and know there is hope for everyone who believes. Will you share what you have received? Will you give away what you have received by grace?

Discouragement is all around us more than ever before. Discouragement is the anesthesia the devil uses on a person just before he reaches in and carves out his heart. When we lose hope, we lose the ability to dream, and despair replaces joy. Somehow, fear replaces faith, and anxiety replaces prayer. Insecurity replaces confidence. It is a crazy way to live, but we fall for it. The greatest gift we can give away is hope. Teachers, that student that drives your slap crazy every day needs hope. Parents of a struggling teen, never give up hope. There may be times as a parent when you are discouraged and ready to throw up the white flag. I encourage you to hang on and keep fighting. When you feel overwhelmed, drop to your knees. Pour out your heart to Him when you begin to worry, worship.

**Romans 15:13: "May the God of HOPE fill you with all joy and peace as you trust in Him, so that you may overflow with hope by the power of the Holy Spirit."**

God's Word is so rich. Hope is found in a close intimate relationship with Jesus Christ. He is the source of true hope. Lay your worries, anxiety, and even your children at His feet. Leave all your cares and discouragement with Him and trust Him. When we trust Him, we will be full of hope, even to the point of overflowing.

*Challenge for today:* First, thank God for His grace. Second, commit Romans 15:13 to memory and hold on to this verse. Last but not least, share hope with someone close to you. Share your story with them and tell them how Jesus has changed your life.

# -53-
# Victory in Jesus

I went to bed last night singing an old hymn that I hadn't sung in a long time, and I woke up still thinking about Victory in Jesus. Wow. There is so much truth in the chorus, which goes like this. O victory in Jesus, my Savior, forever. He sought me and bought me with His redeeming blood. He loved me ere I knew Him, and all my love is due Him; He plunged me to victory beneath the cleansing flood. That song takes me back to Pine Bluff Baptist Church in Albany, Georgia, when I received Jesus as my Lord and Savior.

*1 John 5:4: "For everyone born of God overcomes the world. This is the victory that has overcome the world."*

The conquering power that brings the world to its knees is our faith. The person who wins out over the world's ways believes Jesus is the Son of God.

*Romans 10:9: "That if you confess with your mouth, 'Jesus is Lord,' and believe in your heart that God raised him from the dead, you will be saved."*

There is victory in Jesus. I don't know what you are facing today. This world may be wearing you down, and you are feeling frustrated and tired. I encourage you to begin to sing this old hymn repeatedly. Think about the words and realize what this song is all about. If you are in Christ, you are a child of the King. You have been forgiven because of His amazing grace. We have been set free from sin and death, and one day we will spend eternity with Him in heaven. We have VICTORY in Jesus, and we are overcomers. Take your eyes off the world and keep them focused on Jesus. Victory in Jesus.

*Challenge for today:* This may be strange, but google the old hymn, "Victory in Jesus." Take time to read through every verse and meditate on what the song says. Dig into the truth of this beautiful hymn and ask the Lord to speak to you wisdom for your life. Make a list of things the Lord is showing you.

# -54-
# Abide

How many self-help books have you read in this lifetime? We are looking for something to push us to greatness or motivate us to keep growing. If we could be more determined or focused on our goals, there would be nothing we could not accomplish, right? How often have we started on a project, were highly motivated and enthusiastic, and quit because we were overwhelmed and discouraged? Think about it, what about that project of painting the house or fixing your old truck? It may be something God has placed in front of you to do and started good, but it wasn't as easy as you thought it would be. Then you laid that dream or vision from God to the side. We all get tired and discouraged sooner or later. We find that discipline and stubborn will are insufficient to complete the task.

> **John 15:5: "I am the vine, you are the branches. He who abides in Me, and I in Him, bears much fruit; for without Me you can do nothing."**

We can get involved with many religious activities, but we have difficulty inviting God into the deepest parts of ourselves and practicing His presence. When we attempt to accomplish God's work or even live a Christian life, apart from an authentic relationship with Him, we get burned out and frustrated and fail. God created us for fellowship, so any ongoing work flows naturally from a relationship with God. We tend to grit our teeth and exert our willpower. We wrestle with ourselves, trying to do the right thing when our focus should not be on doing, but on being. It should not be about struggling but abiding. Fruit is never the product of willpower. It's a result of abiding in the Vine. Here is some good news for many of you. Don't try harder to make it happen; rest in what He's already done. Allow the Holy Spirit to flow through you, and let it happen. Lord, I trust You with my life.

*Challenge for today:* Get plugged into the eternal power source of the Holy Spirit. A power that never runs out. Learn to rest in His presence and enjoy the refreshing power of His love and grace. Commit to starting every day off by spending alone time with the Savior of the world. Ask Him to carry your burdens and give you the power to walk in Christlikeness throughout the day. Get yoked in Christ and abide in His presence.

# -55-
# Can You Take a Punch?

I know this is a strange way to start a devotion, but when I was a young boy, I loved to fight. It was all about the competition and the struggle. It was about pushing through pain and suffering and seeing who would outlast the other in this challenge. Yes, I had to take a few good punches along the way and keep pressing forward. But the older I get, I want nothing to do with any fight or wrestling match. We who are older tend to pull something just by tying our shoes. Here are the questions for today. Can you take a punch? How do you respond when life pops you in the mouth? What is your tendency when hard times come your way? Do you keep fighting, or do you roll over and give up?

**2 Corinthians 4:8-9: "We are hard pressed on every side, yet not crushed; perplexed, but not in despair; persecuted, but not forsaken; struck down, but not destroyed."**

"Lord, I know if you bring me to it, you will bring me through it." Men and women of God will face trials, hard times, and suffering. God takes us through those tough training times and uses them to bring about His character. How we respond to them reflects our trust in Him to produce perseverance, character, and hope. King David could take a punch. What got him through many tough times was how he strengthened himself, not in people, not in getting encouragement from friends but in the Lord. David's only hope was in the Lord his God. He wrote Psalms 25:20 and said:

> **"Keep my soul, and deliver me, let me be not ashamed, for I put my trust in You."**

Sometimes our biggest battle is to believe God is with us when those hard times come. During those times, there are no easy answers. We must keep on fighting. We must set our feet, take courage, and believe God is real, alive, and working His purpose in us.

*Challenge for today:* Pray a simple prayer. "Lord, help me to embrace the struggle. Please show me how to have peace during my trials and strengthen myself in you. Help me to trust you when the storm winds begin to blow." Amen.

# -56-
# Obey God Even When It Doesn't Make Sense

Take time to pause and reflect on your life for a moment. Try to recall when God asked you to do something that didn't make much sense at the time. When I was young, I feared talking in front of people. I didn't want to stand before people and share anything with anybody. Then I was asked to be a director of a particular Sunday School department. Without asking any questions, I said yes. It couldn't be that much to do. I could do many things behind the scenes and take all the Sunday School teachers' attendance records. Later I found out that the Director of that department also had to speak in the assembly before all the classes broke out into smaller groups. I think God set me up. It didn't make sense then for me to say yes, but it sure does now. God blesses obedience. I was taking my first step.

I encourage you to read John 2. Take your time, and don't rush through the many truths of God's Word. Here in John 2, we find Jesus and his mother attending a wedding when the wine ran out. This is not a good thing. Can you see the wedding planner rushing around to figure out what to do? It would help if you remembered that, in those days, there were no local curb stores where you could jump in your car and be right back. Mary felt so bad for the wedding party and the wedding planner.

***In John 2:3, Mary says to Jesus, "They have no wine."***

In other words, "Jesus, do something." Even though Jesus hadn't started his public ministry yet, Mary knew who Jesus was. Boldly and without hesitation, Mary directed the servants to listen to Jesus and do whatever He told them to do, even if it didn't make sense. Do it anyway. Jesus instructed them to gather jars together and fill them with water. Remember, there was no running water, so you had to go to a water source or a well and bring the water back to the ceremony. Not an easy task, but they did exactly what Jesus asked them to do. When they got everything in place, Jesus asked them in John 2: 8:

***"Now draw some out and take it to the master of the banquet."***

How crazy was that? I know the servants had to think, this guy will get us fired. Yet one of the amazing parts of the story is that they obeyed. Here is the question, what's He saying to you? Are you willing to follow Him even when it doesn't make sense? If you know that God loves you, you should never question His direction. It will always be right and best.

*Challenge for today:* Pray this simple prayer. "Lord, help us to hear Your voice and obey You even when we don't know the outcome." God is calling you to be a willing vessel even when it doesn't make sense. Trust Him; He wants the best for you.

# -57-
# The Secret Place

How busy is your life? Think about all the different things you have going on right now with work, raising kids, hobbies, and church activities. Our calendars and planners are so full that it has become impossible to keep up with everything that is going on. Life has become a balancing act trying to juggle all the appointments. We rarely have time to sit back, rest, and enjoy relationships in this fast-paced life. Sometimes we need to take a vacation and step away from the routine of life. That time of rest, solitude, and relaxation is what we need to keep going strong.

There is something about Matthew 6:6 that jumps out to me. It says,

**"But when we pray, go into your room and shut the door and pray to your Father who is in secret."**

Where do you go to find solitude and to get intimate with the Lord? I don't know about you, but the business of life, family, and work can wear you down. Too often, the pace of life has paralyzed the power of our prayers. So often, we neglect our time alone with God, and we slide into a life of contentment. We are happy with just existing and getting by. It doesn't have to be like that. Ignite your faith today. I encourage you to find your secret place to get alone with God, away from all the distractions. That includes your cell phone. It needs to be just you and God. We all need this time every single day. The secret place is where all pretense is gone, and there is just a raw, direct intimacy with your Creator. It's where you can be honest and authentic with the Lord. It is a place where you can cry and weep out loud. Even Jesus needed time alone with God. In Luke 5:16:

**"Jesus often withdrew to lonely places and prayed."**

Jesus made it a priority to be recharged by being alone with his Father. What about you?

*Challenge for today:* Find your secret place and allow God to fill you with love, grace, and mercy. People will take notice that you have been with Jesus. Get fully charged. Slow down, take a deep breath, and enjoy the presence of God. It will help you to get through that busy day.

# -58-
# Renew Your Mind

Satan is alive and well. Just look at our world today. Do you see all the confusion, destruction, and lies that seem to be everywhere? There is more hate and dissension than ever before. Churches are struggling to keep the doors open, and finding gospel ministers is getting harder. Satan knows that his time is short, and he is doing everything he can to destroy you. He is raising all kinds of chaos, leaving many broken relationships in his path. We are right in the middle of one of the greatest spiritual battles, and we are unaware of it. Beware of what is happening around you in the spiritual realm, and guard your mind against the attack of Satan.

In the Christian life, the greatest battle is for the mind. Paul writes to us in Romans 12:2:

**"Be transformed by the renewing of your mind."**

Why? Because the enemy is a liar. All he wants to do is deceive and destroy you. When the battle for our mind begins, it starts with destructive ideas, doubts, and fears. Satan's goal is to make those lies take root and become a stronghold in your life. A stronghold is a pattern of thinking that becomes set in our mind, and we convince ourselves it is true even when it's not. It can lead to addictions, depression, fears, and unhealthy habits. Strongholds always start small and grow fast if we are not careful. The good news is that we don't have to live like this.

***2 Corinthians 2:4-5:** "For the weapons of our warfare are not carnal but mighty in God for pulling down strongholds, casting down arguments and every high thing that exalts itself against the knowledge of God, bringing every thought into captivity to the obedience of Christ."*

Strongholds bind, but truth sets you free. Freedom comes by immersing yourself in truth and renewing your mind.

*Challenge for today:* Take time to identify a possible stronghold that exists in your life. Be honest with yourself and with God. Be aware of how Satan attacks you. Spend time talking and listening to the Lord. Lay it at His feet and begin to live in freedom. Dive into the Word and allow it to speak to you. I pray that the peace of God will cover you.

# -59-
# Courage

Who are your heroes of the faith? Who do you look up to when it comes to your faith? What about them sticks out, and what makes them different from everybody else? Make a list of men and women you have always loved and adored in the Old Testament. Then list what it is about them that draws you to them. Some of my favorites are Moses, Daniel, and Ruth. Do the same with those characters in the New Testament. Yes, go ahead and think about whom you enjoy reading about. Whose faith grabs you, and whose life challenges you the most?

Last but not least, who are those modern-day heroes of the faith? Now, what is one of the characteristics you can find in each one of these heroes of the faith, whether they are from the Old Testament, New Testament, or modern day? Personally, for me, it is courage. I see courage in every one of my heroes of the faith, and it is something I need more than anything in my life.

Tony Dungy once said, "Courage is the ability to do the right thing, all the time, no matter how painful or uncomfortable it might be. It takes courage to say "no." It takes courage to stand up for your convictions.

***Joshua 1:9: "Have I not commanded you? Be strong and courageous. Do not be afraid; do not be discouraged, for the Lord your God will be with you wherever you go."***

I don't know what you are facing now, but I understand that life can get tricky. Through it all, God has called us to make a stand. Know today how much God loves you and walks with you every step of the way. Raise up with courage today. Face that giant in your life and say, "I have had enough." Make your stand for Christ and stand with courage.

*Challenge for today:* Thank God for those in your life who have displayed unmeasurable courage and have lived out the Christian faith no matter the cost. Pray for those people, pray a blessing over them, and ask the Lord for courage and strength. Stand firm, Church, and do not back down.

# -60-
# Staying in God's Word

*Psalms 119:1-2: "Blessed are they whose ways are blameless, who walk according to the law of the Lord. Blessed are they who keep his statutes and seek him with all their hearts."*

God's Word is rich and full of truth. He has laid a buffet table before us and is calling us to eat. Come and eat all you want and be full. Do you want to be blessed? Then dive into God's Word. Do you want to be wise? Then spend time in scripture. Look at Psalm 119:9-12:

*"How can a young man keep his ways pure? By living according to your word. I seek you with all my heart; do not let me stray from your commands. I have hidden your word in my heart that I may not sin against you. Praise be to you, O Lord; teach me your decrees."*

The writer of Psalm 119 knew the importance of knowing God's Holy Word, but he didn't stop there. He continues in Psalm 119:24-27 and writes,:

*"Your statutes are my delight; they are my counselors. I am laid low in the dust; preserve my life according to your word. I recounted my ways, and you answered me; teach me your decrees. Let me understand the teaching of your precepts; then I will meditate on your wonders."*

His word is a lamp to my feet and a light for our path. What are you tripping over today? What are you stumbling over in life? God's word will save you a lot of hurts, pain, and wasted time. I encourage you to stay deep in God's Word, especially when Satan throws lies. The one thing Jesus used when he was tempted was scripture. If Jesus needed to know scripture to fight Satan, how much more do we need the Holy Word? God's Word will kill the lies of Satan. Satan can't change who we are, but only who we think we are. I pray that you set your gaze on Jesus. Constantly remind yourself that God made you wonderfully and beautifully. I don't know what is going on in your life. We all have those seasons of life when we don't understand why we are struggling. Sometimes we even question God and ask why. In these times, go back to the truth. Don't forget that God loves you, and you can trust Him. Church, we can't roll over and be content. We must wake up and see that eternity is at stake. Turn the focus off yourself and fall to the Holy One on your knees. Get back into the Word today. It will change your perspective.

***Challenge for today:*** Make God's Word a priority in your life. The more you dig, the greater the treasures you will find. Begin to pray for wisdom and understanding, but don't just study the Bible. You must apply it and live it out. Your life will be transformed, and your heart will be renewed.

# -61-
# Love

How many of us understand what real love is? We live in a world that always talks about love but doesn't comprehend true love. It's not about loving a pair of shoes because they look so good on you. We use the word love to describe how much we enjoyed our vacation or how good our food was at dinner. How would you express love if asked to write it on paper? I want to define love by quoting a very familiar verse, John 3:16:

*"For God so loved the world that he gave his only Son, that whoever believes in him shall not perish but have eternal life."*

God loved us so much that He willingly gave us His Son to die on an old rugged cross to pay my debt for my sin. True love sacrifices, gives unselfishly and forgives. Love is a powerful word, and our generation has the wrong definition. Love is not a feeling; it's a decision. Decisions should not be based on emotions because feelings change. I know I am guilty of letting emotions dictate my mood and how I react to situations far too often. But I need to take a step back and look at the Creator and definition of love, Christ. Seeing it in Scripture is the key to believing Christ's love for us.

*1 John 4:16: "And so we know and rely on the love God has for us. God is love. Whoever lives in love lives in God, and God in him."*

He is constant and unchanging, just like his love for us. Being loved by Christ is the ground for becoming loving in all your relationships. Believing the depth of God's love for me is the key to my growing into a caring person. Putting this into action will only develop all my relationships. When deeply rooted in Christ's love for us, all our relationships will flourish. Stop looking for love in the wrong places. Christ's love is the constant; once we understand this, everything else will fall into place.

*Challenge for today:* Thank God for His amazing love. Praise Him for His never-ending passion for us. Grow deep in your relationship with the God of the universe. Embrace His love, and then give it away.

# -62-
# What is Your Identity?

When I was young, I loved to play sports. You would never see me without a ball in my hand or dirt on my face. There wasn't much sitting around on a couch, staring at the TV and playing video games. I gathered with my friends as much as possible to play a game of football, basketball, or baseball. During the summers, we would play from sunup to sundown, and we only stopped when my mom called us in to eat. Then I rushed through the meal as fast as possible, so I could get back to playing ball. Then I was introduced to the world of organized sports. My passion for playing ball grew from there, and I couldn't get enough. If I couldn't find someone to practice with, I would spend hours shooting a basketball, kicking a football, or hitting rocks with an old broom handle. With all the practice and determination came awards, recognition, and attention. Being an athlete became my identity. When it came time to stop playing ball and get a real job, I lost my identity as an athlete. So, I had to ask myself, who am I? Why has God placed me on this earth, and what is my purpose for living?

***John 1:1-3: "In the beginning was the Word, and the Word was God. He was God in the beginning. Through him all things were made; without him nothing was made."***

God's Word is so deep. I want you to ask yourself a question. Take some time to answer this the best way you can. What is your identity? Who are you? That is a serious question to answer first thing in the morning. Just don't read over it and push the question to the side. Please write it down and ask yourself repeatedly. God poured His heart into creating you and is proud of what He made. He formed us uniquely and purposefully. He knows every detail about us. We put all our identity into earthly variables that will leave us feeling broken and empty. We constantly define ourselves by the wrong things. We listen to the lies of Satan that tell us we are not good enough, not smart enough, and not skinny enough. Today, we tell Satan, "I am through listening to you."

*Challenge for today:* Ask yourself this question. Whom does God say you are? What does God think of you? Sit there and wait for an answer. Don't get in a hurry, and patiently wait for the Father to share His heart with you. Start living life with a purpose and passion. Discover your identity in Christ.

# -63-
# The Gospel of Jesus Christ

God had a plan. He planned to have an intimate love relationship with us. Sin entered the world when Adam and Eve chose to listen to the lies of Satan, but God made a way to restore that relationship. He sent His Son Jesus, that was born of a virgin. Jesus lived a very short life here on earth but without sin. He was tempted in many ways but didn't fall for Satan's schemes. He was the perfect Lamb of God. My Jesus willingly laid his life down on an old wooden cross. He suffered, bled, and died for us. What an amazing love. He was buried in a borrowed tomb, but that tomb could not hold him. Three days later, he overcame sin and death. Praise God, my Jesus is alive and well, and I have proof due to the Holy Spirit living in me.

Put your right foot on the cross of Christ. Put your left foot on the empty grave. Church, stand up for the Gospel of Jesus Christ and share it with someone who needs to know the King.

*Romans 3:23: "All have sinned and come short of the glory of God."*

We all have messed up, and we all have sinned.

*Romans 6:23: "The wages of sin is death, but the gift of God is eternal life through Jesus Christ our Lord."*

*John 14:6: "Jesus said, "I am the way and the truth and the life. No one comes to the Father except through me."*

Check out what Revelation tells us in 3:20,

*"Here I am! I stand at the door and knock. If anyone hears my voice and opens the door, I will come in and eat with him, and he with me."*

Because of that, I have a life. "Thank you, Lord, for joy, peace, love, and abundant life found only in Jesus Christ." Do you know my Jesus? Trust Him today.

*Challenge for today:* Ask him to forgive you of your sin and all your mess-ups. He is faithful and just and will forgive you. Answer the knock and open the door to a new life you never dreamed possible. Jesus came in and took over. If you are already a believer in Christ, I challenge you to share this Good News with everybody you know. Don't be ashamed; don't be afraid, but joyfully share the difference Christ has made in your life with those around you.

# -64-
# Conduits Not Tools

A few months ago, I got a call from my mom. She explained that their water was not flowing very strongly and knew something had to be wrong. My dad began to look around outside and noticed water bubbling up from the ground just outside their back door. I went over to help dig up the water pipe. After an hour of digging, we found where the roots of a tree had busted the two-inch water pipe and stopped the water flow. The next hour was spent cutting away the roots and getting a new pipe to connect the water pipe back together. We turned the water back on, and the water began to flow again. That was some hard work, but thank God for good neighbors. We had all the right tools and plenty of help, and we were able to get the job done.

God wants conduits, not tools. It's not about our abilities or skills but more about our willingness to be used by God. It's more about allowing God to work through us. It's more about us becoming a clean conduit where the work of the Holy Spirit can flow through us. We have often allowed roots and dirt to clog up our conduit from the Lord. Sin will stop the work of the Holy Spirit in your life and cause a lot of heartache and work. Find the source of the problem and give that to the Lord. My dad knew the source of the problem that day. A huge tree had to go. We didn't need to go through that again. Be that conduit that water can flow through to touch a community.

*Challenge for today:* Identify the roots that are growing around you. What are the things in life that stop the flow of the Holy Spirit in your life? What earthly passions or sins are hindering your walk with Christ? Take time to confess these sins and desires to the Lord and ask Him for forgiveness and grace. Ask God to remove those roots of selfishness, pride, and evil and clear the way for sweet fellowship with your Heavenly Father. It will save you many headaches.

# -65-
# Walking In the Light

*John 10:10: "The thief comes only to steal and kill and destroy; I have come that they may have life, and have it to the full."*

That thief is Satan himself. He is called a thief because he will hit you when you least expect it or try to run you over when you are not looking. He will come into your home and rob you blind if you let him. All he wants is to cause pain, suffering, and destruction in your life. He walks in the shadows and waits for his chance to pounce on you and attack your weaknesses at the most inopportune time. His heart desires to see us fall into sin because he knows we serve a holy God. He wants to do everything he can to break that fellowship with your heavenly Father. Be on your guard and get ready to fight. The closer you get to Christ, the stronger the light of truth becomes and the easier it is to expose sin and deceit.

*1 John 1:8-9: "If we claim to be without sin, we deceive ourselves and the truth is not in us. If we confess our sins, he is faithful and just and will forgive us our sins and purify us from all unrighteousness."*

Through the Word of God, the indwelling Holy Spirit shows the Christian that he still possesses an old nature and needs the forgiveness of sins. The blood of Jesus Christ is the divine provision for both. To walk in the light is to live in fellowship with the Father and the Son. Sin interrupts fellowship, but it cannot change that relationship. Confession restores fellowship, and immediate admission keeps the fellowship unbroken. This is so important. Search your heart if you seem miles away from God and have not heard God's voice in some time. See if there is something that you need to get right with your Heavenly Father. Walk in the Light.

*Challenge for today:* Take time to confess your sin to the One who died for you. He is faithful. He will forgive you and restore that fellowship. What are you waiting on? Stop what you are doing and make this your number one priority.

# -66-
# Romans 10:14-17

My former youth pastor, friend, brother-in-law, and mentor, Billy Durham, gave me a book for Christmas. It is called "Not God Enough." J. D. Greear wrote it. You need to read this book because it will open your eyes to see how big God is big. He is bigger than we can ever imagine and more significant than our words describe. God is big enough to handle all our questions, doubts, and fears. He wants to take us from our boring faith to a new, vibrant, growing faith. God is infinite and holy, and when we experience His presence, he won't just change how we think; it will change how we live. It will change the way we share our faith.

> **Romans 10:14-17: "How, then, can they call on the one they have not believed in? And how can they believe in the one of whom they have not heard? And how can they hear without someone preaching to them? And how can they preach unless they are sent? As it is written, 'How beautiful are the feet of those who bring good news!'"**

We owe the gospel to others. Let that sink in. The greatest injustice in the church happens when those who know the gospel don't share it with those without Christ. As Christians, we are commanded to go and make disciples of all nations. The greatest question is no longer if you are called, only where and how. 2 Peter 3:9 tells us that God is unwilling that any perish. No, not one. His will for the lost helps me to understand his will for my life. Where God sends you is up to Him, but whether he has called you is settled. Our God is vast and will give you everything you need to share the Good News.

*Challenge for today:* Understand that our God is big. Spend time talking with the Father about where He wants to send you. Next door? We must share the Good News of Jesus Christ! Be confident and know He is with you and will give you the words to share. Live out your faith and trust our BIG God!

# -67-
# Missionary or Imposter?

I love Paul's heart for people. He was a man on a mission. Yes, I see Paul as being loud, bold, and always speaking up without thinking it all the way through. Because of his faith in Jesus, Paul faced significant opposition and mistreatment. In Acts 14:18-19 they stoned Paul and left him for dead, but he kept preaching Jesus. The persecution kept coming in Acts 16:22-24:

> *"The crowd joined in the attack against Paul and Silas, and the magistrates ordered them to be stripped and beaten. After they had been severely flogged, they were thrown into prison, and the jailer was commanded to guard them carefully. Upon receiving such orders, he put them in the inner cell and fastened their feet in stock."*

That didn't stop Paul from sharing his faith, but it fueled him to keep on sharing about the love of a holy God. You see, Paul wasn't an imposter but a true missionary in every sense of the word.

Charles Spurgeon once said, "If Jesus is precious to you, you will not be able to keep your good news to yourself. You would whisper it into every child's ear; you would be telling it to your husband; you would be earnestly imparting it to your friend; without the charms of eloquence, you will be more than eloquent; your heart will speak, and your eyes will flash as you talk of this sweet love. Every Christian here is either a missionary or an imposter." Wow!

> *2 Corinthians 5:14-15: "For Christ's love compels us, because we are convinced that one died for all, and therefore all died. And he died for all, that those who live should no longer live for themselves, but for him who died for them and was raised again."*

I want to make sure you caught that. Paul said, "If you are in Christ, we should no longer live for ourselves but for the one who died for us." I am so full of myself. How about you? We are more passionate about our workout or a room we just painted than our Lord Jesus Christ. It is sad to say, but this is the truth. When we genuinely love God, we want to tell others about His amazing love and grace. Missionary or imposter?

*Challenge for today:* I challenge you to share your story of how God has changed your life with two people. We cannot keep this Good News to ourselves. I pray that you are so full of Jesus that you begin to spew over and get Jesus on everything you touch.

# -68-
# Isaiah 53:4-6

*Isaiah 53:4-6: "Surely he took up our infirmities and carried our sorrows, yet we considered him stricken by God. But he was pierced for our transgressions, he was crushed for our iniquities; the punishment that brought us peace was upon him, and by his wounds we were healed. We all, like sheep, have gone astray, each of us has turned to his own way; and the Lord has laid on him the iniquities of us all."*

The beauty of the gospel is that the One who has the right to condemn us has also made provision for our forgiveness. Do we take His love for granted? God made way for us to have abundant life through His Son, Jesus Christ. Get down on your knees and praise Him for His provisions. Thank Him for His grace, mercy, and incredible love. He was pierced for our sins; he was crushed for our iniquities. The Lord has laid on him the iniquities of us all. We must share the good news of Jesus Christ because Jesus is the way, the truth, and the life. No one comes to the Father except through Jesus. That is the TRUTH.

J. D. Greear said, "To be loved without being known feels shallow, and to be fully known without being loved is rejection. The cross of Jesus is the answer to our dilemma. When we expose our souls to Him, he receives us, forgives us, cleanses us, and saves us. In his eternal love, we find the well for which our soul has been searching." What a wonderful Savior. What a mighty Redeemer. He bore the sin of many and made intercession for the transgressors. He died for you and me, and he took the punishment for our sins. He willingly laid his life down on an old, rugged cross at Calvary. The Good News is this, that grave could not hold him, and sin could not stop him. Our God is alive and well, and He lives in my heart. Do you know my Jesus? Have you experienced his love and mercy? Today is the day of salvation. Call out to Him and receive His amazing love.

**Challenge for today:** Take extra time and read the entire chapter of Isaiah 53. Then praise Him with all your heart and thank Him for all He has done for you. Worship Him and enjoy His presence.

# -69-
# Let's Be Real

What mask are you wearing today? If we were honest, we would all put up fronts to other people to say we have it all together. We never want people to know that we are struggling or have difficulty adjusting to different circumstances. I want you to be honest with me. What fear are you facing? Are you dealing with rejection and hurt? Is there an addiction you are fighting, and all seems hopeless? Is there a broken relationship that needs mending? Are you hiding from God because you have gotten so comfortable? Life has a way of getting the best of you. I encourage you to write a note telling God exactly how you feel. Tell Him what you are facing. Then read it out loud to Him. Then say, "I need you."

God has a better plan for you to live in victory. Hebrews 12:1-2:

*"Let us throw off everything that hinders and the sin that so easily entangles, and let us run the race with perseverance, the race marked for us. Let us fix our eyes on Jesus."*

When we face fear, we must remember to trust in our Creator. We need to worship when we worry and become overwhelmed with anxiety. We need more than religion. We need an intimate and personal relationship with the great I Am. You will never be alone.

*Challenge for today:* Come clean and be honest with your Heavenly Father. Walk in victory, not because of your great wisdom or charm, but because of who you are in Christ. Overcome. Our hope is found in Christ. Thank God for His provision, and give Him glory for what He is doing in your life.

# -70-
# What Are You Full Of?

Y ou must be careful answering this question. What are you full of? This is a critical question because you are usually full of the overflow of your life.

**_Romans 15:13: "May the God of hope fill you with all joy and peace as you trust in Him, so that you may overflow with hope by the power of the Holy Spirit."_**

There are so many things that we fill our lives with. We fill our lives with material wealth like new clothes, nice vehicles, and expensive toys. We also run after power, position, and prestige. The things and hopes of this world will not satisfy and will leave you HOPELESS. God wants the very best for you. The God of hope and joy can provide that in you if you trust Him.

**_Colossians 3:5-8: "Put to death, therefore, whatever belongs to your earthly nature: sexual immorality, impurity, lust, evil desires, and greed, which is idolatry. Because of these, the wrath of God is coming. You used to walk in these ways, in the life you once lived. But now you must rid yourselves of all such things: anger, rage, malice, slander, and filthy language from your lips."_**

What Paul is encouraging you to do is to put to death whatever belongs to your earthly nature.

Confess your sins to the Father and ask Him to cleanse you. Ask for that healing in your life, but don't stop there. Not only do we need to strip ourselves of sin and worldly lust, but we also need to put on the things of Christ.

> **Colossians 3:12-14: "Therefore, as God's chosen people, holy and dearly loved, clothe yourselves with compassion, kindness, humility, gentleness and patience. Bear with each other and forgive whatever grievances you may have against one another. Forgive as the Lord has forgiven you. And over all these virtues put on love, which binds them all together in perfect unity."**

When the pressure of this world squeezes you, what comes out? What are you full of today? Fill yourselves with the things of God.

*Challenge for today:* I urge you to pray to the Lord and say, "Kill me and then fill me." Ask Him to strip you of anything that is not pleasing to Him and confess your sins before His throne of mercy. Ask Him to purge you from all unrighteousness and shame. Then ask Him to fill you with goodness, peace, joy, and all the goodness of the Lord. Fill yourself with Jesus; when the world squeezes you, Jesus will get on everything you touch.

# -71-
# God, Take Your Time

We live in a fast-paced world, and it is not slowing down anytime soon. These days, fast food is not fast enough. Let's face it; we hate waiting for anything and expect to be served immediately. Have you ever asked the question, what is taking so long? As a child, I used to love going to theme parks and riding all the rides, but today I avoid going to any theme park at all costs. Think about it; you must wait in line to get into the parking lot. Then you wait in line to get a ticket to the park. Then you wait in line to get a ten-dollar drink so you can cool down when you stay in another line to ride a ride finally. So much waiting.

> **James 1:4: "Perseverance must finish its work so that you may be mature and complete, not lacking anything."**

Perseverance and patience are not one of my strongest traits. How about you? We live in a world where we want everything now. We do not want to wait on anything. Traffic drives me crazy. I want to get from point A to point B as fast as possible. I don't have time to wait. The weekend seems like it will never get here, and I wish my days away. I pray for the anointing of the Lord to reach thousands of people for Christ, and sometimes I become very frustrated. Perseverance does take its time. I have learned over the years that God knows what He is doing and has a plan and purpose for all the waiting. Trust Him.

Pray this challenge prayer, "Lord, take your time. Take your time with me and help me be all you want me to be. Lord, make me content in the place you have me. Please help me not wish my days away but live with purpose and passion every day. Slow me down to enjoy friendship and take no opportunity for granted. Lord, I still pray for that anointing, but I realize You don't have that much to work with. Take your time, Lord. Help me to enjoy the process of becoming more like You."

*Challenge for today:* Slow down. Take time to enjoy God's goodness and the blessings of life. Don't rush through this life, and wish your days away. While you wait, be faithful, and take the time to praise Him. Waiting gives you time to rest.

# -72-
# Proverbs 4:26-27

*Proverbs 4:26-27: "Make level paths for your feet and take only ways that are firm. Do not swerve to the right or the left; keep your foot from evil."*

What road are you traveling on?

*Matthew 7:13-14: "Enter through the narrow gate. For wide is the gate and broad is the road that leads to destruction, and many enter through it. But small is the gate and narrow the road that leads to life, and only a few find it."*

You may be at a crossroads here today, and a battle is going on inside your mind. Which road do you go down? You have a choice of which path you walk down; choose well.

This is worth repeating, make level paths for your feet and take only ways that are firm. Do not swerve to the right or left; keep your feet from evil. This life is a long journey, and Satan has been known to set out a trap or two along the way. He is very creative and is willing to do anything to discourage you and pull you off the path God has for you. One of his favorite traps is to influence our thinking. Incredibly, two people can look at the same picture but have different perspectives. One will see exceptional beauty or find something positive. The other person will see something different. All they see is the negative and what is wrong with the picture. We all have various weaknesses and strengths, but we must recognize how Satan attacks us as individuals. The most important thing to do to stay on the right path is to keep your eyes on Christ. He will lead you and guide you through the traps and snares. Trust your guide. Listen to His voice and follow his instructions closely. Satan wants to do everything he can to sidetrack you and distract you from the path God has called you to walk.

*Challenge for today:* Say no to negative thinking. Guard your heart. Stay focused on the road ahead, and keep your eyes on your guide no matter how familiar the road may be. The enemy is waiting for you when you least expect it. Please keep it on the road and choose well.

# -73-
# Beat Up?

***Acts 21:30-32: "The whole city was aroused, and the people came running from all directions. Seizing Paul, they dragged him from the temple, and immediately the gates were shut. While they were trying to kill him, news reached the commander of the Roman troops that the whole city of Jerusalem was in an uproar. He at once took some officers and soldiers and ran down to the crowd. When the rioters saw the commander and soldiers, they stopped beating Paul."***

You could say that Paul was having a terrible day. You may not be physically pulled out of your house and beaten half to death, but some days we can comprehend what Paul went through. Life can rough you up pretty well at times.

We all face rejection, disappointment, and heartache in this life. Have you ever felt like you can't catch a break, and nothing seems to go your way? David had those seasons in his life too. Life can run over you, hang you upside down, and slap you around. How do we overcome it? It's not enough to walk yourself through, grit your teeth, and keep walking. We all have been told that we are not intelligent, handsome, or qualified. With all this going on, have you ever wondered how we could accomplish God's purpose for your life? Yes, it does take grit at times to keep going. David knew something about enduring and walking through life.

*Psalms 139:13-14: "For you created my inmost being; you knit me together in my mother's womb. I praise you because I am fearfully and wonderfully made; your works are wonderful, I know that full well."*

When you felt beat up and rejected, immerse yourself in the acceptance of Christ. He has created you for a reason and a purpose. You are fearfully and wonderfully made. God made you, and you have a purpose to fulfill. Keep your eyes on Christ and run after Him with all your heart. Stay focused on the truth and turn your back on the lies of Satan. Remember, you are the child of the King. Live like it.

*Challenge for today:* Rest in the presence of God and enjoy His company. Put away the cares and worries of this world. Say this out loud repeatedly, "I am fearfully and wonderfully made." Let His love go deep today and receive the joy He gives to His children. God bless you and your walk with Him today.

# -74-
# Comfort

There are times when I am alone with God, and He encourages me and motivates me. But there are some days God steps on my toes. Today is one of those days. One of the giants I face in life is comfort. I never saw this as a problem until today. Most of us desire to be comfortable. We like to stay in our zone and not rock the boat. I want to stay with what is familiar and safe. How about you? Faith is confidence in what we hope for and assurance of what we do not see. That doesn't sound comfortable to me. The cross brought pain to Jesus in the same breath; it brought freedom to us. We are alive today because of Christ's discomfort on the cross.

**2 Corinthians 12:10: "For Christ's sake, I delight in weakness, in insults, in hardship, in persecution, in difficulties. For when I am weak, then I am strong."**

Faith thrives in discomfort. Many of us are guilty of gathering in our churches and hanging out together in our comfort. While the Goliaths of this world shout and intimidate us, we stand by like David's brothers and do nothing. Lord, help me to have a heart and passion like David. "God, make us strong and help us to live a life that brings You glory, even if it makes me uncomfortable. Move us, God."

Look at what God said to Abram in Genesis 12:1:

*"Leave your country, your people and your father's household and go to the land I will show you."*

Think about this; God asked Abram to take off and leave everything he held dear to his heart, yet He didn't tell him exactly where to go. He couldn't make any plans. I am sure Abram was thinking, what do I tell my family why I am leaving? Where will I land, and how will I make a living? In other words, God was asking Abram to get outside of his comfort zone and place his total trust in Him. God continued to talk to Abram in Genesis 12:2-3:

*"I will make you into a great nation and I will bless you: I will make your name great, and you will be a blessing. I will bless those who bless you, and whoever curses you I will curse, and all the people on earth will be blessed by you."*

God blesses obedience. Even though it didn't make sense to Abram then, Abram obeyed God's request.

**Challenge for today:** Take time to sit down with God. Search your heart and ask yourself some difficult questions. Ask yourself, am I walking in the center of God's will for my life? Am I using the gifts that God has given me to serve other people? Am I walking according to what God has called me to do, no matter the cost? Give God your 'yes' today.

# -75-
# Romans 6:8-10

**Romans 6:8-10: "Now if we died with Christ, we believe that we will also live with him. For we know that since Christ was raised from the dead, he cannot die again; death no longer has mastery over him. The death he died, he died to sin once for all, but the life he lives, he lives to God."**

Jesus died one time for all time. His work was completed. He overcame sin and death, and death was swallowed up in victory. Didn't you know Satan was celebrating when Jesus died on that old rugged cross, but he began to tremble when Jesus arose from that grave three days later? My Lord and Savior, Jesus Christ, is alive and well today, and because of that truth, I can experience joy, peace, and His amazing love. I want you to understand something. Satan has been defeated, yet he is still dangerous.

**1 Peter 5:8: "Be alert and of sober mind. Your enemy the devil prowls like a roaring lion for someone to devour."**

Satan hates you, and he wants to do everything he can to destroy you. I know many people who love the Lord and are believers in Christ. They want to live for Him, yet they still deal with giants. The good news is that we are not left alone with anything to fight with.

149

**James 4:7: "Submit to God. Resist the devil, and he will flee from you."**

We are to stand against temptation, and we are to lean into the all-sufficient One. By sufficient, I mean that Jesus is enough. He is able. Jesus has overcome and is fully competent. He is the One who fights our battles. We are to align ourselves with the person and work of Jesus Christ. Yet, we must remember that Christ brings down the giants, not us. How often do we still function like killing the giant is all on us? So many times in life, we thank God for saving us, but we tell God I will take it from here. If we are to have real change in our lives, we must understand our dependency on the all-sufficient Jesus. Our evolution is more about trusting and less about trying.

*Challenge for today:* Memorize First Peter 5:8 and hold it close to your side. Be aware of Satan's temptations and traps that he will set along your path. Stay far away from sin and keep focused on the promises of God. Keep your eyes on Christ. You have victory because of what Jesus did for you over 2,000 years ago. Thank Him for His saving grace.

# -76-
# Face Your Giant in Front of You

Facing a giant can be a scary thing. Just ask the children of Israel. In First Samuel chapter 17, Goliath taunted God's army repeatedly. The children of Israel were overcome with fear and did not face their giant until a young boy named David had enough. He decided to do something about it; David met his giant face-to-face. I love what David told Goliath in First Samuel 17:45-46:

> *"You come against me with sword and spear and javelin, but I come against you in the name of the Lord Almighty, the God of the armies of Israel, whom you have defiled. This day the Lord will hand you over to me, and I'll strike you down and cut off your head. Today I will give your carcasses of the Philistine army to the birds of the air and the beast of the earth, and the whole world will know that there is a God in Israel."*

You know the rest of the story. David killed the giant and led Israel to victory. If God is for us, who can stand against us? We serve a mighty God.

What Goliath are you facing today? It may not be a nine-foot giant like what David faced, but it is just as real. Maybe you are facing a giant called fear. It can leave you shaking in your boots. Perhaps you are terrified of rejection or fighting some form of addiction. Whatever it may be, the question remains. How do I get rid of the giants? Jesus offers abundant life to everyone who follows him. John 10:10 tells us this truth today:

> *"The thief comes to kill, steal, and destroy. But Jesus came to give us life and have it more abundantly."*

Jesus intended for us to really live. That means we can live freely in the power of what he has accomplished for us. Whatever giant we're battling might be big, but it's not bigger than Jesus. There is hope in Jesus Christ.

*Challenge for today:* Identify what causes fear and be willing to write it out. Share that with a dear friend. Present this fear to the Lord and be ready to lay it at the feet of Jesus. When fear rises in your spirit, say aloud and speak God's truth, "Greater is he that is in me than he that is in the world." Face your giants head-on, and don't run away because you are an overcomer in Jesus Christ.

# -77-
# I Dare You to Pray This Prayer

Growing up as a little boy in Southwest Georgia, I enjoyed playing outside. We only came in when we had to eat or get cleaned up to go into town. We could spend the entire day building tree houses and forts in the woods. Of course, we would have our trusty BB guns at our sides for protection. If we were not playing in the woods, we would play some ball with all our neighborhood friends. To me, there was nothing more fun than that. Yes, we would play from sunup to sundown. I also remember riding bikes through the woods and all over our neighborhood. We would also build ramps with spare boards and blocks that we found lying around. The bigger the ramp, the higher we could get in the air. After we gathered all the materials we could find, we began constructing the biggest ramp we could build.

Was it built with high quality and safety in mind? I would say no. But the following words out of our mouths were, "I dare you to jump it." Who had the guts to jump this massive ramp and live to talk about it? If there were no takers, we would say, "I double-dog dare you." You couldn't dare let a double-dog dare go by. Typically, one of us would answer the call.

I have a double dog dare for you today. Paul prays a beautiful and powerful prayer over the Church in First Thessalonians 3:12-13:

*"May the Lord make your love increase and overflow for each other and for everyone else, just as ours does for you. May he strengthen your hearts so that you will be blameless and holy in the presence of our God and Father when our Lord Jesus comes with all his holy ones."*

He prayed that the Lord might increase their love and overflow for each other and those around them. How would that change our church and our neighborhood? He doesn't stop there, but he goes on to pray to strengthen their hearts so that they will be blameless and holy in the presence of our God. What a prayer. I pray for a soul that will be blameless and holy in the presence of my Father. I pray that His love will overflow and get on everything I touch. How can we give away what we don't have? I double-dog dare you to pray this prayer for the Church of Jesus Christ.

*Challenge for today:* I challenge you to pray for your local body of believers for seven days. Record what God does around you in the life of others but also in your life. Don't be scared to pray this prayer several times a day.

# -78-
# Ever Lost Your Focus?

It is so hard to be vulnerable and authentic with people. It is so hard at times to let people see the real you. We don't want people to know our weaknesses or shortcomings. What would people say, or what would people think of us if they knew the real us? I sometimes want to put a mask on and make people think I have it all together. I hate to admit it, but the truth is I start so good on a project or a task, and as time passes, I lose focus on what I am supposed to do. Other things become more important, and I become distracted from the task. This morning God pushed a word directly in front of my face. Don't you love it when God does that? He tells us today, "Don't lose focus on what is most important."

*1 Corinthians 10:31: "So whether you eat or drink or whatever you do, do it all for the glory of God."*

This world has a way of distracting us from what is most important. Have you ever lost your focus on Christ and the ministry that He has called you to? The distraction of death, business, bills, and everyday life can pull your focus away from the passion God has placed in you. I encourage you to stop whatever you are doing and tell God exactly where you are. Be honest with Him. Revelation 2:3-5 Jesus tells the church at Ephesus this:

*"You have persevered and have endured hardship for my name and have not grown weary. Yet I hold*

*this against you: you have forsaken your first love. Remember the height from which you have fallen! Repent and do the things you did at first. If you do not repent, I will come to you and remove your lampstand from its place."*

Return to your first love and your former devotion to Christ. Keep your eyes on Christ and stay focused on his will for your life.

*Challenge for today:* Ask yourself a question, am I living life for the glory of God, or am I just getting by? I have been in a holding pattern, but God is doing work in my heart. "God help me to take my eyes off myself and help me to live out my calling to reach people for Jesus Christ. For your glory." Keep the main thing, the main thing.

# -79-
# Face Discouragement Head On

Discouragement can knock you to your knees. I don't care who you are or what your name is. We all face it, and it sometimes gets the best of us. It's like having a slow leak in your car tire. It's no big deal, and you can stop and get some air, but your warning light goes off three days later. Now it is starting to get on your nerves. The leak seems to worsen as time passes, and you must stop more often. Have you ever noticed there is never a good air pump around when you need one? Sometimes it's better to go ahead and take care of the problem in the beginning before it gets worse. Satan wants the church to be discouraged, but I want to give you something to fight back.

> **Psalms 37:4-7: "Delight yourself in the Lord, and he will give you the desires of your heart. Commit your ways to the Lord; trust in him and he will do this: He will make your righteousness shine like the dawn, the justice of your cause like the noonday sun. Be still before the Lord and wait patiently for him; do not fret when men succeed in their ways when they carry out their schemes."**

When you are pushed into the corner of discouragement, fight back. Delight yourself in the Lord. Come into His presence and worship Him. You must take your eyes off yourself and focus on the true love of God. Then He will give you the desires of your heart. Stay true to what the Lord has told you. When discouragement comes, we begin to doubt God and His promises. Be still before the Lord and wait patiently for him. God's heart is to deliver, delight, and develop you.

*Challenge for today:* Don't get backed into the corner of discouragement. Come out swinging and overcome the scheme of Satan. When discouragement begins to pile up, set aside time to spend with the Lord and worship, enjoy His presence, and know that the King of the universe loves you, don't be scared to tell the Lord what is going on in your heart and mind. He wants to hear from you.

# -80-
# Distance Respect or Intimate Relationship

In Exodus chapter 20, God handed down the Ten Commandments to Moses. He laid it all out plain and simple. Exodus 20:18-19:

*"When the people saw the thunder and the lightning and heard the trumpet and saw the mountain in smoke, they trembled with fear. They stayed at a distance and said to Moses, 'Speak to us yourself and we will listen. But do not have God speak to us or we will die.'"*

Moses was a great leader who encouraged the people not to be afraid. But the people remained at a distance. So often, we prefer distant respect over an intimate relationship. Please take time to read James 4:7-10. Dig in and pull out the truth that will encourage you. Submit yourself to God, resist the devil, and come near to God. It will be the greatest decision you ever make.

There is an old saying that I have heard my whole life: *Stuck between a rock and a hard place.* Sometimes that can describe life. We have all experienced that in life. If not, hang on because it is coming. Moses knew precisely what we were going to face. In Exodus 14, Pharaoh began to pursue Moses and the children of Israel. The nation of Israel was terrified. If that wasn't enough, the Red Sea was in front of them. They were stuck between a rock and a hard place. What would they do? How would they survive? Why were they going through this? Do those questions sound familiar?

> *In Exodus 14:13-14, Moses said to the people, "Do not be afraid. Stand firm and you will see the deliverance the Lord will bring today. The Lord will fight for you; you need only to be still."*

Those are the words that you may need to hear today. Stand firm and be still. Let the Father fight for you. How much energy do we waste trying to figure it out or worrying over something we can't control? God not only has your back but also is preparing the road ahead. God is good.

*Challenge for today:* God is calling you to come close to Him. He desires a close intimate relationship with you and not a distant respect. God wants to speak to you and share great and exciting truths daily. Can you grasp that great word and receive that? Give yourself entirely to God and place your life in His hands.

# -81-
# One Decision Away

Life is a grind, and so many times, we get lost in it. 2018 was one of those years for my family and me, that is for sure. How often do we get tied up in our day-to-day routine and find ourselves just trying to make a living? We are just going through the motions of life. I encourage you not just to make a living. Make a life. Make a difference. You don't need to change jobs, and you don't need to change your circumstances. You don't even need to change friends. The good news is this: you are one decision away from a different life. One decision. It's incredible to look at the lives of Jacob, Joseph, Moses, and Samuel. They were great men of God, and God did some amazing things through their lives and their ministries over the years. They all had one thing in common. They all said, "Here am I." They all made themselves available to God and held nothing back. What are you waiting on? You see, our job is to be available anytime, anyplace.

God doesn't do what God does because of us. God does what He does despite us. All we must do is stay out of the way. Stay humble. Stay hungry. If you aren't hungry for God, you are full of yourself. There have been times in my life and ministry when it was all about me. I was doing a lot of good things for the wrong reason. Over the years, God has opened my eyes to the selfishness and pride that covered my heart. Then the Lord gave me the scripture from John 3:30:

**"He must become greater; I must become less."**

That word has changed my heart and ministry forever. Give God control of your life. Die to yourself and watch what God can do.

*Challenge for today:* Memorize John 3:30 and repeat it aloud throughout the day. Ask the Lord to reveal the selfishness and pride in your heart and life. Then take time to get those things right with your Heavenly Father. Then I challenge you to tell the Lord, "Here am I; use me for your glory."

# -82-
# Favor Of God

I love the truth found in the story of Noah. Genesis 6:5-6:

*"The Lord saw how great man's wickedness on the earth had become, and that every inclination of the thought of his heart was only evil all the time. The Lord was grieved that he made man on the earth, and his heart was filled with pain."*

Even though God's heart was breaking because of the sinfulness of mankind, He still had hope. In Genesis 6:8:

*"Noah found favor in the eyes of the Lord."*

In times of great wickedness, one man stood out. One man endured and walked with God. Look at Genesis 6:9:

*"Noah was a righteous man, blameless among the people of his time, and he walked with God."*

Noah had the favor of God in his life. The favor of God is what God can do for you that you can't do for yourself. It's His favor that opens doors of opportunity. It's His favor that turns opposition into support. So how do you find favor? It's obedience. It's obedience to the voice of God in one's life.

***Genesis 6:2 2: "Noah did everything just as God commanded."***

Noah carefully listened to God's instructions and followed every little detail God gave him. He didn't go off by himself and devise a great plan to build an awesome boat. God gave him details in Genesis 6:14-21 on how to make this boat. God told him exactly what He wanted him to do. God gave Noah a colossal task: building a boat in the desert. This whole process took a total of 120 years. This wouldn't be accomplished overnight, but it would take faithfulness, discipline, and commitment. This was not a sprint but a marathon. Noah had first to take a massive step of faith and trust that he heard the voice of God. Look what Genesis 7:5 says again about Noah:

***"And Noah did all that the Lord commanded him."***

God blesses obedience. Obedience starts by surrendering our lives to the lordship of Jesus Christ. If we don't hold out on God, God will not hold out on us. We also position ourselves in favor of God by walking in humility and purity. If we want to discover new lands, we must lose sight of the shore.

*Challenge for today:* Don't be scared to ask for God's favor. Just know, He may put a huge task before you and ask you to follow His plan completely. Take time to listen to His instructions. Then pray for wisdom and discernment and follow through with complete obedience. Don't forget that God never gets in a hurry and is always on time.

# -83-
# Enjoy the Walk

Life is a journey. There will be hard times in this life, and you will face trials and temptations along the way. Many times, I find myself turning molehills into mountains. I try to figure this crazy life out, and I worry about how I will handle certain situations. I fret about what people think of me because I focus on the problem or the difficult situations. I find myself living in fear and doubt. When things seem to fall apart or life isn't going as planned, discuss it with the Lord first. Don't let your focus be on the problem but on the Lord Jesus. Don't allow inconvenience, frustration, and disappointment to shape your day. It is easy to get distracted by Satan's schemes and things that don't matter.

*Proverbs 3:5-6: "Trust in the Lord with all your heart and lean not on your own understanding; in all your ways acknowledge him, and he will make your paths straight."*

Trust in the One who made it all. Know that our God is faithful and cares about all the intimate details of our lives. Don't forget that you are a child of the King, and you are dearly loved and cared for. Have complete confidence today that He is going before you and preparing the way. Life is like walking up a mountain. It's steep and slippery sometimes, and you will meet things along the way that make you want to turn around and return. Situations and circumstances in this life can make you question God, and you may not understand why things turned out a certain way. Keep trusting, and don't turn back. Life is a journey; some steps will be harder to take but learn how to enjoy the walk. He takes every step with you and will carry you during those difficult times.

*Challenge for today:* I encourage you to keep pressing on. Don't look back, and keep your eyes on Christ. Let your walk with Him be honest and intimate. It will make your journey up the mountain worth it. The beauty at the top of a mountain is breathtaking. Enjoy your walk with the Father.

# -84-
# Grace is Enough

I have a message I want to share with you. You're not perfect. That may come as a shock, but it is the truth, and we all know it. We all have our imperfections, and it's okay. There is only one who walked this earth and remained perfect. His name was Jesus. We want to paint a picture to the world that we have it all together and we have everything under control. But there will be times when we get knocked down and feel overwhelmed. We have all been there and have experienced it. Look at some of the greatest Christian men in the Bible, like Peter, who denied Christ three times. How about Paul being beaten, whipped, and thrown in prison multiple times? That had to be a tricky thing to go through, especially when you know you are doing the right thing.

*Thank God for Second Corinthians 12:9: "My grace is sufficient for you, for my strength is made perfect in weakness. Therefore, I will boast all the more gladly about my weakness, so that Christ's power may rest on me."*

For so long, we have looked at trials and failures as things that can break us. We need to see the beauty, joy, and strength God can bring out of difficulties. I know it's easy to write about but hard to live out. Thank God for His grace today. Think of it as God's riches at Christ's expense. He has never promised us a trouble-free life, but He did promise He would be there through all of life's situations and struggles.

He will never leave or forsake us, especially in the difficulties. Hold on to His promises. His grace is enough. I want to leave you with a word of encouragement found in First Thessalonians 5:16-17:

> **"Be joyful always; pray continually; give thanks in all circumstances, for this is God's will for you."**

*Challenge for today:* Take time to thank God for His never-ending grace. Don't dwell on your shortcomings or all the times you have messed up in this life. Tell God how grateful you are for giving us so many do-overs and how He loves us no matter what. Say out loud today, "Your grace is enough." Be joyful, pray continually, and thank the Lord for life's blessings.

# -85-
# Friend of Sinner

Middle School was an incredible time in my life. My buddies and I had such a good time. We were always playing games in our spare time. I remember the fun of wallball before school. We would go to the homeroom, and there was no telling what we smelled like, but we didn't care. Then came lunchtime; we would run to the lunch line to eat our food, then rush outside to play football.

Another thing that pops into my mind is that we all had nicknames. I've mentioned before that my buddies and I called each other by our mama's name. We thought it was hilarious to dig and find out what our mama's name was. I was known as Linda all through my sixth-grade year. Being known as Linda passed, that fad passed away quickly. Around that eighth-grade year, I was sweet about someone who eventually became my wife, so I had to get her attention. So, I came up with a new haircut, the butt cut. Yes, this haircut was going to change my life forever. I parted my hair right down the middle of my head and sprayed it down with hair spray. I wanted to let the world see the new me, so I decided to go to the men's church league softball game and display the new hairstyle. As soon as I walked up, everybody noticed, and my new nickname was blurted out, "Slick." That name stuck with me till my twelfth-grade year. My nickname communicated something about me, about how people saw me. What people call you says a lot about how they perceive you.

Jesus was called many names; all he did was love and help people. Many of the religious leaders of that day were jealous of his success. They wanted to discredit him in the eyes of the public. So, they said all sorts of crazy things about him. They accused him of being demon-possessed, a rioter, and a threat to public peace.

**Luke 7:34: "The Son of Man came eating and drinking, and you say, 'Here is a glutton and a drunkard, a friend of tax collectors and sinners.'"**

In their minds, this was meant to hurt him. This was meant to get under his skin and cause Jesus grief. The logic was. If Jesus hung out with the wrong people, He must be terrible too. But for Jesus, the title "Friend of Sinners" was a sign of success, not shame. Here is what we must see as Christians. Relationships come first; change comes later. Unfortunately, many believers mix up that order. We try to correct people before we connect with people. Every Christian has a past, and every sinner has a future in Jesus Christ.

*Challenge for today:* Before we judge someone or put someone down, don't forget what God has forgiven you for. Reach out to people and befriend them for the very reason of winning them to Christ. Do it the Jesus way, and don't worry what other "church people" may say.

# -86-
# Matthew 9:9-13

I have two questions I want to ask you to think about today. First, what was Jesus' message when he walked the earth in human form? Secondly, who was the message for?

> *Matthew 9:9-13: "As Jesus went on from there, he saw a man named Matthew sitting at the tax collector's booth. 'Follow me,' he told him, and Matthew got up and followed him. While Jesus was having dinner at Matthew's house, many tax collectors and 'sinners' came and ate with him and his disciples. When the Pharisees saw this, they asked the disciples, 'Why does your teacher eat with tax collectors and 'sinners'? On hearing this, Jesus said, 'It is not the healthy who need a doctor, but the sick.' But go and learn what that means: 'I desire mercy, not sacrifice.' For I have not come to call the righteous, but the sinners."*

Matthew met Jesus, and his life was changed forever. Before he met Jesus, Matthew wasn't nice. He was more like a Mafia boss than an IRS employee. At that time, Rome was the world power, and the Roman army was brutal and barbaric. They would kill the men, rape the women, and enslave the children. After conquering new territory, the Roman government would impose taxes on the local subjects. That's where Matthew came in. His job was to collect taxes from his own people. Yes, he betrayed his people. But here is the kicker: Tax collectors were required to turn in a certain amount of money to Rome, but they could keep anything they collected above that. So, they extorted money from their people. The Jews hated tax collectors and were known as traitors, thieves, and bullies. Is that someone you want to hang out with? That is why it's so startling that Jesus made friends with people like Matthew. He didn't just talk to them; Jesus loved them. What qualified this "Gangster" to be a disciple of Christ? Jesus called him, and he followed just like that.

Sometimes we make it too difficult for people to follow Jesus. Jesus doesn't wait for us to clean ourselves up or renounce our lifestyle. He finds us where we are and calls us to follow Him. You see, Jesus' message was grace. It was salvation for all who believed in Him. Jesus himself was the message. The message isn't mere doctrine; it is not about behavioral change. The message is that no matter who you are or how badly you've messed up, grace and forgiveness are available in Jesus.

*Challenge for today:* Share this devotion with a friend, then share your story about how Jesus has changed your life.

# -87-
# Finding the Pharisee Within

eligion seeks to control, impress, and confirm. You see, religion is more concerned about outward behavior than inward change. It values performance and perfection. The Pharisees were the golden standard of holiness in Jesus' day. They were also arrogant, mean, and very self-righteous. Instead of showing mercy and leading people to God, they condemned and discouraged people. Jesus regularly called the Pharisees out for their judgmental attitudes and used terms like blind fools, snakes, and hypocrites. Take time to read Matthew 23:16-33 today and see where Jesus spoke directly to the teachers of the law and the Pharisees.

> **Matthew 23:13: "Woe to you, teachers of the law and Pharisees, you hypocrites! You shut the kingdom of heaven in men's faces. You yourselves do not enter, nor will you let those enter who are trying to."**

The crazy thing is, they didn't mean to be this way; they thought they were pleasing God. The Pharisees missed Jesus' point. Here is the truth, apart from Jesus, there is no such thing as "a good person." With Jesus, there is grace, wholeness, and life. That is good news.

> **Romans 6:23: "For the wages of sin is death, but the gift of God is eternal life in Christ Jesus our Lord."**

It's not about religion; it's about a relationship.

***Challenge for today:*** Are we judgmental, and do we try to impress others with our good deeds? Do we have a Pharisee spirit within us? Thank God for His amazing grace, and guard your heart against judging others. Come before the throne of grace and confess your shortcomings to your Heavenly Father.

# -88-
# Mark 10:17-22

*Mark 10:17-22: "As Jesus started on his way, a man ran up to him and fell on his knees before him. 'Good teacher,' he asked, 'what must I do to inherit eternal life?' 'Why do you call me good?' Jesus answered. 'No one is good except God alone.' You know the commandments: 'Do not murder, do not commit adultery, do not steal, do not give false testimony, do not defraud, honor your father and mother.' 'Teacher,' he declared, 'all these I have kept since I was a boy.' Jesus looked at him and loved him. 'One thing you lack,' he said. 'Go, sell everything you have and give to the poor, and you will have treasure in heaven. Then come, follow me.'"*

Here is a person who, in everyone's eyes, had everything, and most people would call him a success. Yet, he still felt like he was missing something. He was empty, and he had questions he couldn't answer. Have you ever met someone who seems to have made it, but he is living in torment in real life? You can have all the great things this world offers and still be empty. So many people live their whole life climbing the ladder of success, and when they get to the top, they figure out they have climbed the wrong ladder.

The rich young ruler had underestimated Jesus. He heard the rumors that Jesus was the Messiah, the coming Savior, and God in the flesh, but he wasn't ready to call him

Lord. He wasn't prepared to admit that the man in front of him was God. So, he played it safe and called Him a 'good teacher.' Many people want Jesus to be a part of their lives, but they don't want Him to be the Lord of their lives. He had questions, and he needed some answers. The rich young ruler wanted to know how to make it to heaven and find fulfillment. He had followed the church's rules and was a great guy to everyone. Then Jesus responded, "Sell all your stuff and give it away, then follow me." Then comes the saddest scripture in the Bible, found in verse 22. The rich young ruler went his own way and didn't follow Jesus. You see, he was asking for medicine instead of a miracle! Jesus came to transform hearts and lives. He is bigger than our good deeds, and he is greater than all our sins too. God is for you and has an awesome plan for your life. Do you know him? Have you ever received him as your personal Lord and Savior? Today is the day to walk in newness and peace.

*Challenge for today:* Identify what you are holding back from the Lord. Be willing to go all in and surrender everything to his control. Allow him to sit on the throne of your heart, and let him rule and reign in your life. He loves you deeply and wants to give you his best.

# -89-
# Who Is Carrying the Load?

How many carry emotional, spiritual, and mental burdens beyond our abilities? We all do this at certain times in our lives. How does that affect our emotions, our relationships, our thought processes, and all our decisions? In Matthew 11:28-30 Jesus tells us this:

> *"Come to me, all you who are weary and burdened, and I will give you rest. Take my yoke upon you and learn from me, for I am gentle and humble in heart, and you will find rest for your souls. For my yoke is easy and my burden is light."*

In other words, God wants to carry the heavy weight for you, and He does that through Jesus. How often do we feel worn out, tired, and in pain? Not because God is asking too much of us but because we insist on carrying too much. God knows all about our oversized egos and our undersized strength.

Ask yourself, what unnecessary weight are you carrying today? Is it: yesterday's burdens, blunders of your past, or sins that you can't get past? You must know this; your failure does not frame your future. Think about all the great men and women of the Bible who messed up, but God still chose to use them greatly. Look at the life of Paul. He was known as a Christian killer, and the people in the church feared him. Then in Acts 9, Paul met the Lord, and that encounter changed his life forever. Imagine the guilt and shame that Paul faced, but after he met the Lord, he experienced grace and forgiveness. Jesus came to carry what we could never shoulder on our own. No matter what weight you are struggling with, Jesus can take it for you. The answer isn't to work harder, sleep less, or plan better. The answer is found in the person of Jesus Christ. Jesus is telling us to stop working on our own and to work with him instead. His yoke keeps us attached to Him. His yoke keeps us in step with Him, and He keeps us pointed where He is going. Taking His yoke upon us isn't about pulling more weight; it's about letting Him pull our weight. When we are yoked up to Him, everything changes. We will accomplish things we never thought possible because we are yoked to the supernatural power of Jesus. We were created to walk together with Christ, and we will find rest when we do.

*Challenge for today:* Get yoked with Christ. In other words, connect to the Lord and let Him carry your heavy load. What do you need to lay out the feet of Jesus? Trust Him with it today.

# -90-
# Trust?

**1 Peter 5:6-7: "Humble yourselves, therefore, under God's mighty hand, that he may lift you up in due time. Cast all your anxiety on him because he cares for you."**

This verse doesn't just tell you to cast your cares on God; it tells you why you can cast your cares on him. "Because He cares for you." To trust someone can be a scary thing to do. We sometimes have trouble trusting God to do a better job caring for us than we could. Most of us have been let down by other people more than once, so we have learned to look out for number one. God cares about your friendships, He cares about your family, and He cares about your marriage. Yes, all those little things that most people don't even pay attention to; He cares about that too. Are you convinced that God cares for you? Until you are convinced, you will never cast your cares on Him. I want to share great news: His love doesn't run out. His affection, mercy, and grace never end.

Have you ever thought that letting Jesus carry the load is only for the weak? We don't need to do life in our own strength, and we don't need to do our fair share. We are called as Christian believers to cast our cares on Him. That sounds simple, but casting takes effort, and we must be intentional about it. Casting is a decision we must make when life slaps us in the face or begins to overwhelm us. What weights are you trying to carry by yourself, and what burdens are you trying to shoulder alone? It's time to transfer all your cares and concerns to the only One who can hold it all. Yoke up, connect to your heavenly Father, and go in the same direction. Take time to learn of God, trust Him, and listen to His voice.

> *1 Peter 5:10: "And the God of all grace, who called you to his eternal glory in Christ, after you have suffered a little while, will himself restore you and make you strong, firm and steadfast."*

Trust Him with it all and walk in freedom and confidence—yoke up.

*Challenge for today:* Memorize First Peter 5:6-7 and say it repeatedly. Ask God to open your eyes to those things that hold you captive and weigh you down. As He reveals these burdens and worries to you, write them down and spend extra time talking with your Father about them. Commit to spending more time with Jesus and growing in that relationship today. As you grow in that relationship, you will begin to trust Him at a different level. Leave all your cares at His feet and trust Him with it all.

# More Books By Dennis Taylor

1. **Fuel For Today; Volume 1. A 6-Month Devotional Guide For Spiritual Growth And Encouragement**
2. **The Total Package**
3. **Fuel For Today; Volume 2. A 3-Month Devotional Guide For Spiritual Growth And Encouragement**
4. **Surrendered; From Stressed To Blessed; Your Best Life In Jesus' Easy Yoke.**

# About the Author

I started in Student Ministry when I was twenty years old, and it has been my calling for nearly thirty years. My heart was for students to come to know Christ and to grow in their relationship with Him. I love to see God's light bulb fill their eyes and hearts, and I loved sharing the Gospel of Jesus with students whom everybody else said were a lost cause. My passion was to teach them about a relationship with the Lord and give them a real-life example of what it looked like to be walked out in everyday life. My time alone with God has always been my rock, fortress, and high tower. Spending time praying each morning, reading God's Word, and listening to His voice has changed my life forever. I love sharing with young believers who dare to dive deep into the river of God's love. It is so rewarding to invest in the life of other people, watching them go from the shallow end of faith and dive into the deep water of a love relationship with Jesus.

I had the privilege of pastoring two churches, which greatly blessed my family and me. First, the Lord led us to plant a church in Leesburg, Georgia. It was a time of growth and a time of great joy. I loved preaching God's Word weekly and encouraging and loving families. We started with twelve people in our home one Sunday morning; a short time later, God opened the door to purchase a building on a couple of acres in Lee County. That church is still going strong and is known as Forrester Community Church. I also had the privilege of pastoring Salem Baptist Church in Worth County, Georgia. Salem is a small country church with a huge heart for God and its community. I was there for a short time, but they have a very special place in my heart.

Today, I serve as the Pastor of Sports and Recreation at Park Avenue in Titusville, Florida. Peter Lord was the founding pastor of Park Avenue Baptist Church. He was also the author of several well-known books such as Hearing God, Soul Care, 959 plan, and many more. In addition, he was one of the greatest communicators of God's Word I have ever heard. I had the honor of being discipled by this great man of God back in 2004 as the Senior High Student Pastor. My role today at Park Avenue is to use sports and recreation to reach out to the community around us. As we develop relationships through sports, God opens the door to share our Jesus with them and their families. My hope, joy, and calling are to lead as many people as possible into a saving relationship with Jesus. Then encourage them to take those next steps to grow and mature in their faith.

In 2022 I wrote two devotional books, Fuel for Today Volumes One and Two. I also penned the book The Total Package, which deals with living a balanced life in Christ. My last chapter book is called Surrendered. I married Laura, my high school sweetheart, and we have been happily married for 36 years. The Lord has blessed us with two grown kids; Carsen serves at Passion City Church in Atlanta, Georgia, in the Children's ministry. Mackenzie serves in the sports and recreation ministry at Warren Baptist Church in Augusta, Georgia.